I'm Good Enough,
I'm Smart Enough,
and Doggone It,
People Like Me!

Also by Al Franken

Rush Limbaugh Is a Big Fat Idiot

I'm Good Enough, I'm Smart Enough, and Doggone It, People Like Me!

DAILY AFFIRMATIONS BY STUART SMALLEY

Really by Al Franken

A Dell Trade Paperback

A DELL TRADE PAPERBACK

Published by
Dell Publishing
a division of
Bantam Doubleday Dell Publishing Group, Inc.
1540 Broadway
New York, New York 10036

ISBN: 0-440-50470-8

Printed in the United States of America

Published simultaneously in Canada

November 1992

20 19 18 17 16 15 14 13 12 11

BVG

I'm Good Enough, I'm Smart Enough, and Doggone It, People Like Me!

To myself, Stuart, whose *experience* I wouldn't trade for any other human being's (although I've had some pretty horrendous experiences), whose *strength* grows little by little, day by day, and who *hopes* this book will be a huge success!

The first time I met Stuart Smalley, who describes himself as a "caring nurturer and a member of several twelve-step programs," it was late one Saturday night. Dateless, I was home, doing the next best things—telling myself that was *okay*, because I loved *myself* and watching *Saturday Night Live*.

I was partly thinking about my life, and partly scanning the television hoping the Church Lady would come on, when I saw Stuart. He was at a Weight Watchers meeting, trying to twelve-step them (a recovery term meaning "convince, enlighten, help, attract, share with") into Overeaters Anonymous.

"Hello. I'm Stuart, and I'm an overeater," he said.

"This isn't O.A. and we don't do that here," the group leader said back.

Stuart replied that he was aware of that, but he liked it when people said "Hi, Stuart."

The group said "Hi, Stuart."

A short time later, he confronted one of the group members about keeping the focus on herself, saying that was something he had learned in O.A.

Then he acknowledged that he had lost weight at Weight Watchers—4 pounds. But he quietly and immediately followed that with the fact he had lost 127 pounds in O.A.

Later, when the group became upset upon learning that the scale was miscalibrated and everyone weighed three-quarters of a pound more than they had been told they weighed at "weigh-in," Stuart suggested saying the Serenity Prayer, like they did at O.A.

Quietly, deliberately, with the innocence of a child—an adult child—Stuart pestered his way through the meeting, and into my heart.

For a moment, I stopped thinking about my life. This is about *recovery*, I thought.

If imitation is the highest form of praise, maybe the next best is being the subject of a *Saturday Night Live* skit.

The next time I met Stuart was at Teacher's Too, a restaurant on New York's Upper West Side. Stuart, via his creator, Al Franken, talked about his plan to write a daily meditation book. Later, after asking me to write this preface, he started sending me portions of the book.

I found myself devouring the pages of what a meditation book reflects: a year in the life of its writer. I watched Stuart begin his journey by wondering how he could possibly write a book, then watched him spiral into shame when he decided he couldn't.

I watched his struggles with self-esteem, shame, and acceptance.

I delighted in his efforts to let go, and his constant reminders to himself to be clear on what he could, and couldn't, control.

I particularly enjoyed his bouts of "taking to his bed"— sometimes for days and weeks at a time—when things became too much for him.

Stuart spent the year going through contortions to feel his feelings, and to feel his feelings about his feelings. He had bouts of anger, followed by flurries of amends. He plunged, periodically, into complicated feelings about his family members. He struggled with friendships, and with his beliefs about spirituality and how *he* understood his Higher Power.

He listened to his friends, and he tried not to judge them when they behaved or believed differently than he did.

He worked hard not to judge himself.

As soon as I'd finish one batch of meditations, I would eagerly begin awaiting the next.

Once, when I had taken to my bed during a particularly debilitating bout of sadness, I picked up Stuart's book and started reading. Before long, I was giggling. Then it was only moments till I was up and running again.

Stuart's book helped me heal myself.

I can remember back in the old days, before recovery books really existed. We had the Bible and the Big Book of Alcoholics Anonymous, but that was about it. Little groups of us would pass around photocopied sheets of paper with little blurbs and bits of wisdom and information, and we were happy to have those.

Now, we have tiered sections in bookstores.

And I'm happy we have that many choices about reading matter that can assist us on our journey.

When I participated in a panel at the American Booksellers Association Convention in Las Vegas, Nevada, in 1990, I talked about this new recovery genre in literature, what it meant to me, and where I thought it was headed. I said I believed recovery books were books that educated, inspired, encouraged, and helped people in their transformation process.

I also said I believed it was important not to limit recovery books to traditional forms.

It's important for them to be entertaining and well written. In fact, I said, those elements may become a necessity.

Stuart's meditation book meets all the criteria.

In all his struggles and innocence and sincerity and dedication, Stuart made me laugh. He helped me see myself in a new light. He gave me hope.

He helped me appreciate the Stuart in me.

And that's okay.

Melody Beattie

Author's note: Whenever I pick up a book, I know I should read the author's introduction first. But sometimes I just skip ahead and go to the first chapter. And then I feel guilty, and beat myself up. So I'm the last person to want to put you through that kind of horror. But I *really* think you'd get more out of this book if you read the introduction. But you do what you want. It's okay! (Though I think you should probably read the introduction first.)

All my life I've kept hearing the same things over and over again. "Stuart, you're not good enough." "Stuart, you're not smart enough." "Oh, and by the way, Stuart, no one likes you." And do you want to know the worst part? Who do you think was saying these awful things? My Mom? Well, yes. My Dad? Okay, him too. My "special" relationships? Ditto. But mainly, those words were coming from me!

That's right, me. The tiny little Stuart that sits inside my brain criticizing every move I make, every breath I take. In fact, he's there right now, saying, "Hey, you just stole a lyric from a song by the Police." But there's another voice, a new voice inside, saying, "That's okay! Everybody knows it's a Police lyric, so it isn't stealing, because I didn't try to pass it off as my own. And besides, it was very apropos! Good work, Stuart!"

Where did this new voice come from? From a simple *tool, the daily affirmation.* An affirmation is a *positive* statement. The *positive* affirmation *replaces* the old *negative, critical* voice. So the *negative* "You have no idea what you're doing. This introduction sucks" becomes the *positive* "I am a creative person! This is a great introduction!"

Unfortunately, it isn't always that easy. For those of us who grew up in dysfunctional situations, there is a constant struggle between the old negative voice we're familiar with and the new positive voice that can set us free to live a happy and fulfilling life. But that's okay! "Progress, not perfection," as we say in the program.* Look at me! Four short years ago I couldn't get myself out of bed. (Small wonder. I weighed nearly three hundred pounds!) Now, forty-eight months and one hundred and twenty-seven pounds later, *I am writing a book!* Now, that's progress!

But not perfection. This book will not be perfect. Even though I want it to be. Which is my problem—I'm a perfectionist! And that's okay. It's my problem, and I am owning my problem! I'm a perfectionist because somewhere deep down I still don't totally believe that I'm good enough and smart enough, and the only way to prove I am is to be perfect, which is, of course, impossible. So I drive myself nuts. Literally! Well, I refuse to do that with this book!

So I have made a decision. *I will not rewrite!* That's right. Because I realize that if I allowed myself to rewrite this book or any part of this book, any sentence, phrase, or word, I would drive myself stark raving mad *and I would never finish!* So I have made myself a solemn vow. I will write the book *in the moment!* Talking into my tape recorder, as I am right now. One day at a time. One affirmation a day. And I will not change a thing, including this introduction. As I think back, the part about the Police song lyric *is* kind of dumb. But that's okay! It's perfect in its imperfection!

---

* By "program" I mean any one of the twelve-step programs that are based on the twelve steps of Alcoholics Anonymous, which is actually one of the few twelve-step programs I *don't* belong to. I *am* in OA, Overeaters Anonymous, which is for those of us who are powerless over food. Then there's Al-Anon, for friends or family members of alcoholics, which I qualify for in spades. Then there's ACOA, Adult Children of Alcoholics, for adults who grew up with one or more alcoholic parents. Thank you, Dad, for that one. And then there's CoDA, Codependents Anonymous, for people who are codependent. But I find I don't go to that as much, because I like Al-Anon better, and they cover a lot of the same ground. But some people like CoDA better. And that's okay! Good for them! And finally, there's DA, Debtors Anonymous, for those of us with money issues. I know this sounds like a lot, but believe me, I need all the help I can get!

MY SOLEMN VOW

I will finish this book one year from today. Every morning I will exercise, shower, eat a good breakfast, then sit down at my tape recorder, and talk down that day's affirmation. I will not rewrite! What I say into my tape recorder the first time is just fine! Because I'm good enough! I'm smart enough! And doggone it, people like me!

Also, I will get dressed between showering and breakfast.

TODAY I WILL EMBRACE THE CHANCE TO START ANEW!

Okay. That was a mistake. *Every* day is a chance to start anew. And by singling out January 1st, I'm giving the impression that we should live one *year* at a time instead of one *day* at a time. Now I kind of wish I hadn't promised myself not to rewrite. But I did! It's just that I hate starting out on the wrong foot. Maybe this book is one big, huge mistake. But that's just Stinkin' Thinkin' and I refuse to beat myself up! If I could just start over somehow. Oh well, let's move on.

TODAY I WILL THINK OF CREATIVE SOLUTIONS TO MY PROBLEMS!

There. I did it. A few years ago, I would have said to myself, "Stuart, you made a solemn vow not to rewrite. Move on to January 2nd." And that would have been okay. That was me then. This is me now. And the me now (does that make sense?), the me now, Stuart, now, the person that I am now (oh, I wish I could rewrite), anyway, I realized that I had a problem: How can I start over without rewriting? And I, the me now, realized that problems have solutions. And I solved it! Why? Because I didn't give up! Of course, sometimes we *should* give up. When we're trying to do the impossible. Such as control another person. So, forget "I didn't give up!" The real reason I solved my problem was that I believed in myself! That's it! I believe in me!

I BELIEVE IN ME!

Okay. That's a fitting way to start. Say it to yourself. Several times. "I believe in me!" "I believe in me!" At first you might not buy it. You might have a negative reaction. And that's okay! Remember, for your whole life that critical voice inside you has been saying "I don't believe in me! I don't believe in me!" Well, he's wrong! Or she! Okay. That's something I have to figure out. How to deal with the "he" and "she" thing. Okay, I have to stop making mental notes to myself like this. I vowed not to rewrite, and . . . I wonder if I can just omit things? No, then I'd start censoring. . . . Okay, I'm sorry. I've completely forgotten where I am.

I WILL LET GO OF PAST MISTAKES!

I had trouble sleeping last night. Because I was holding on to yesterday's bad start. But then I realized that there was nothing I could do about it, other than try to think of some creative solution to the whole mess. And that kept me up a lot longer. So this morning I was really just dog-tired. I mean, already this book is exhausting me, and it's only January 2nd! Then I remembered to *let go*! Let go! Get off my own back! (I'm heavy enough as it is!) This doesn't mean give up. It just means I don't have to get in my own way. If I let go and let God, it'll be okay. Or as Donna, a woman in my OA group who is totally addicted to waffles, likes to say, *"Leggo my Eggo!"* And it works! She's lost eighty-three pounds and I think this is my best affirmation yet!

I WILL LET GO OF PAST MISTAKES! II

Okay. I did have trouble sleeping again because I realized that I didn't do the best job of explaining "Let go of past mistakes." And let me say that at about 3:00 A.M. I did see the irony. I mean, I'm not an idiot! And I had to laugh. Which I think helped me get to sleep. Anyway, I did explain a little yesterday about letting go, but not about letting go of the *past*. Too often, we live in the past or in the future, and forget that *now* is the only time you can live. But that's okay! In fact, it's more than okay, because if you think of it, *It's always now!* But by living in the past or in the future, you're missing out on life! If I look back at my first forty years on this planet, and take away all the times I was living in the past or the future, I'd say I really existed for maybe a month. So let's live now! And now! And now, now, now, now, now!!!!!

I WILL LISTEN WITH LOVE TO WHAT MY BODY IS TELLING ME.

think I'm getting a cold. Which is my body telling me I have a dis-ease. In other words, I am not at ease, hence, a dis-ease, i.e., my feeling sick is being caused by my ill-at-ease-ness. God, I wish I could rewrite! But I can't; I'd drive myself crazy. Instead, I'm just making myself sick. Which is my body telling me that I'm having one big humongous codependent slip. Which is okay. At least I'm naming it and owning it and saying "Hey, I accept the fact that I'm in a shame spiral, but I still love myself and will keep taking the actions I need to take." Which are: getting up, exercising, showering, getting dressed, eating a good breakfast, and then talking into this tape recorder. It's going to be okay!

TODAY I WILL STAY IN BED IF I AM SICK!

I don't even think that's an affirmation. This whole thing is turning into a total disaster. I can't exercise today. I'll just get sicker. My throat is so sore, I can barely talk. Why did I ever think I could do this?

I AM A FRAUD!

Who do I think I am, writing a self-help book? How can I help other people when I'm this imposter! I mean, I'm not even a licensed therapist! Why did I tell everyone I was doing this book? Boy, talk about setting yourself up! I am disappointing so many people. My friends. My book agent. My editor at Dell. I don't dare show her what I've written. Why did Dell pay me to do this anyway? They can't know what they're doing. No other publisher in their right mind would buy this book. I wonder if I have to give back the advance.

I AM A SUCCESS!

As we start the new year on this the first day of January, January 1st, the first day of the new year, we remove all negative thoughts, and remind ourselves how competent, intelligent, and . . . Who am I kidding? I'm sorry, I give up.

I WILL BOUNCE BACK!

The last five weeks have been pure hell! If I left my bed, it was either to go the bathroom or to eat graham crackers. Or both. I isolated. I didn't call my Al-Anon sponsor, my OA sponsor, my DA sponsor, or my ACOA sponsor. And I don't know if they called me, because I wouldn't answer the phone. I was in total despair. And finally, last night, I realized something. After four years in recovery, not only had I relapsed, *I hit bottom!* And you know what? It's okay! In fact, I'm grateful. Because now that I know it can't get any worse, *I am ready to change!*

TODAY I WILL BEGIN TO CHANGE!

Most of us are afraid to change. God grant me . . . the *courage* to change the things I *can*. And what can we change? I can't change what I wrote in January. Well, I guess actually I can. But that would be rewriting. Of course, I could change my vow not to rewrite. But I still think that would be a mistake. Something I *can* change are my attitudes. For example, my attitude about rewriting. I think that's been my problem. I've never really accepted the fact that I cannot rewrite! Wow! This is a breakthrough! God grant me the serenity to accept that I cannot rewrite!

TODAY I WILL GET WHAT I NEED WITH THE HELP OF GOD, AS I HAVE COME TO UNDERSTAND HIM!

Everybody's understanding of God is different. Joanne, a dancer in my Debtors Anonymous group, believes that God put a parking space in her life. And that's okay. (She was late for a meeting, got a parking spot right in front of the church, and ran in to hear the exact thing she needed to hear.) But my Higher Power doesn't do that type of thing. My Higher Power is the part of me that is connected to everything in the Universe, including Joanne and the trees and the birds and Neptune! And you. My Higher Power loves me and knows what's best for me and when I remind myself to stay in contact with Him (which I really did not do in January), I almost always get what I need. And I don't worry. As my Uncle Frank used to say, "Worrying is paying interest on money you'll probably never borrow." Of course, Uncle Frank was killed on a trip to New York when a crane fell on him.

TODAY I WILL REACH OUT TO OTHERS.

I finally got the courage to show this to another human being. Ray, my Al-Anon sponsor, told me he thought it was good, but that I might be trying too hard. It reminded me of something Lily Tomlin once said: "Why do we always have to try harder? Maybe sometimes we should try *softer*." Jerry, my DA sponsor, said that the stuff I wrote in January was very honest, and that this book could be an inspiration to a lot of sick people if I actually finish it after such a pathetic start. Jerry didn't really use the word pathetic, but I think that's what he meant. Joanne, the dancer who believed God put a parking spot in her life, suggested that I read a couple other daily affirmation books to draw inspiration. What a great idea! Maybe the Higher Power put Joanne in my life!

I WILL NOT DRIVE MYSELF CRAZY BY COMPARING MYSELF TO OTHERS.

took Joanne's advice and looked through Melody Beattie's *The Language of Letting Go: Daily Meditations for Codependents.* And it was beautiful. Of course, I immediately started thinking, "Her book is so much better than mine. She's such a terrific writer. I suck." But that's Stinkin' Thinkin' again raising its ugly head. And I refuse to beat myself up! Comparing ourselves to others is an invitation to our critical inner voice. "Gosh. Critical Inner Voice, I haven't heard from you lately. How do you think I compare as a writer to, say, oh, Kahlil Gibran? Hmmm? Which do you think is more poetic? 'In your longing for your giant self lies your goodness; and that longing is in all of you' or 'I'm good enough, I'm smart enough, and doggone it, people like me'? What do you think, Critical Inner Voice? And while you're at it, who has a stronger profile? Me or Mel Gibson?" I am a human being, and human beings are not perfect. I love everything about me, even my imperfections! Oh, and I read Melody Beattie's meditation on comparing yourself to others, and you know what? I like mine better! But that's comparing, and I shouldn't do that. But I did. And that's okay!

TODAY I CAN CHOOSE TO FEEL GOOD!

Yesterday it dawned on me that maybe this book won't be a huge, horrendous embarrassment. And I started to feel good about it. But this morning I woke up feeling vaguely anxious. And I thought to myself, "Oh, I'm vaguely anxious about the book." But you know what? I don't think that's it at all. I think I'm vaguely anxious about having nothing to be specifically anxious about. I'm uncomfortable being comfortable. My dis-ease makes me un-easy about feeling at-ease-ness. Or something like that. Well, doggone it, that's as stupid as it sounds! I have choices. And today, I choose to feel good! And because I feel good, it's easier for me to accept myself and my faults and the fact that I cannot rewrite. Because this whole thing about feeling un-easy is probably the worst yet. But screw it. If you don't like it, that's your problem! Okay, I'm sorry. I think it's very important for a writer to respect his readers' feelings, and that was just uncalled for.

TODAY I DON'T HAVE TO OBSESS ABOUT VALENTINE'S DAY!

Okay, I think I know what I was vaguely uncomfortable about. Tomorrow. You see, at the moment I have no "significant other." I don't even have an insignificant other! I really haven't felt ready for a relationship since I left Dale, who was a rage-aholic. So tomorrow when everyone else is getting valentines and flowers, guess who's getting a dozen roses from himself? Here's a hint. The card says "To Stuart, forgive me for all the times I did not give you unconditional love. You are the best! Love, Stuart." The FTD man was an Adult Child of Obsessive Gamblers and thought it was the most beautiful note he had ever taken over the phone!

TODAY I WILL MASTURBATE!

Okay, that was a mistake. I should have written "Today I will masturbate—*if I want to!*"

I AM A CENTER OF CALM IN THE EYE OF THE HURRICANE!

My editor, Andrea, called about twenty minutes ago! And I panicked. As soon as I realized who it was, my heart started pounding. When Andrea asked me how it was going, I assumed it was because she sensed that things weren't going that well. For God knows what reason, I thought that if I offered to show her what I'd written, she would then think everything was okay and not ask to see it. Before the words were even out of my mouth, I realized I was making a huge mistake. Of course, Andrea said, "Well, normally I wait until the first draft is done, but if you *want* to show me what you have . . ." Then she gave me her fax number and said she was dying to read it. "Believe me, I need a little inspiration today!" I'm thinking, "Wait till she reads January 7th through February 8th. That ought to inspire her!" Then I told her it might take me a day or two to get the stuff typed up, and she said, "Take your time. Send everything. Don't deprive me of any of your riches." What do I do?!!! I immediately called Ray, my Al-Anon sponsor, but I got his machine. I got Jerry's (DA) machine too. And Carl's (OA), and Fred's (ACOA). Finally, I got Joanne (DA) who told me the Higher Power had made me panic. And then I yelled at her and hung up. That's when I realized I was still out of control, so I looked in the mirror and repeated "I am the center of calm in the eye of the hurricane" six times. And it worked! It calmed me down enough to realize that I am in no state to figure out what to do. Other than write this, which I guess Andrea will be reading very soon. Andrea, I'm sorry I let you down.

I REFUSE TO LIVE FROM CRISIS TO CRISIS!

Which is, of course, how I grew up. My house was *the* original house of High Drama. Of course, we pretended to be Ozzie and Harriet, but believe me, we were really the Addams family, and my dad was It or Thing or whatever. Anyway, we lived from crisis to crisis. And that's what I'm in the middle of now. A crisis! I mean, I have to send my editor the pages. I can't very well tell her my dog chewed them up. I made an amends to Joanne and pointed out that perhaps this is for the best. Maybe I wanted to put myself in this position. Joanne said that's what she meant by saying my Higher Power made me panic, and then she said that I don't have to live from crisis to crisis, which gave me the idea for today's affirmation. So again, maybe God did put Joanne in my life. Anyway, I guess I have to send this to Andrea, my editor. I mean, the longer I put it off, the worse it gets.

I AM AN HONEST PERSON!

I'm so afraid Andrea (my editor) will phone, that I'm screening all my calls with my machine. The program teaches us to be totally honest, so I've changed my message from "Hello, this is Stuart, I am not home right now" to "Hello, this is Stuart, I am unable to take your call at the moment." Then I realized that what's most important is being honest with yourself! *Owning* my own feelings. And to tell you the truth, I mean, to tell *me* the truth, I am petrified. And I know it's because I am acting out my abandonment issues. I am scared stiff that this woman will reject my work, which I'm not that happy with myself, and thus reject *me*. Which, frankly, is why I'm not dating. I have to face this straight on. I have to fax this woman the pages!

I WILL NOT PROJECT NEGATIVELY INTO THE FUTURE!

Last night about midnight I made a decision. *I will fax the pages to my editor today.* I spent the rest of the night lying in bed contemplating my future. Scenarios ran through my head like the bulls at Pamplona. Every scenario was different, except that they all started with my editor calling and ended with me homeless and penniless with no one to love me. Why do I do this to myself?! Mark Twain once said, "I've suffered a lot of catastrophes in my life—many of which never occurred!" How true! How wise! And Twain did not belong to even one twelve-step program! Just imagine if he had!

TODAY I WILL TAKE THE ACTIONS I NEED TO TAKE!

When we live one day at a time, it becomes easier for us to take the actions we need to take, because we know we only have to do what we need to do today. But for some reason I still have not faxed my editor the pages. Jerry, my DA sponsor, offered to fax them for me, if I can't get myself to actually physically do it. Carl, my OA sponsor, suggested I call Andrea, tell her I've changed my mind and would like to wait until I'm finished to show her the book. After all, I am entitled to change my mind! I decided to meditate and establish contact with my Higher Power to find out what I should do. I've never been very good at meditating. I used to just sit there and wonder if I was doing it right. Then I heard someone say that *there is no wrong way to meditate*, and that really helped. Suddenly I was able to empty my mind of all the junk and really listen to what was inside me. Then one day I was meditating and out of the blue like a bolt of lightning this thought came to me: *There must be a wrong way to meditate.* And since then I've been having trouble. But anyway, this morning I closed the shades in my living room, put on a tape of waves breaking onto shore, sat on the floor, closed my eyes, cleared my mind of all thoughts, and sneezed. And that's when I realized that I'm getting another cold, and that if I don't send this woman the pages, I'll never sleep and get really sick. So today, I will take the action I need to take. I will send my editor what I've written so far, and let go of the results.

TODAY I DON'T HAVE TO MAKE UP MY MIND!

Last night I faxed my editor the pages from an all-night drugstore. Actually, it was about two in the morning. I just couldn't get myself to send it while I thought she was there in her office, so . . . Well, anyway, I'm in a coffee shop. I don't want to be home when she reads it. I've been here about two hours now. It's nine o'clock and she should be getting into the office any minute, and I'm just a wreck. Thank God for Carl, my OA sponsor. We had breakfast together (half a grapefruit, coffee with skim milk, and six glasses of water). I told Carl that . . . Just more water, please . . . I'm sorry, that was me talking to the waitress. I told Carl that the pressure was driving me crazy, and that maybe I should just give the money back, and get some kind of job. Carl said that maybe my editor will like the pages, which she should be getting any second. Oh God, it's 9:10 . . . Excuse me, Miss, what kind of waffles do you have? Uh-huh. Let me try both . . . And even if she didn't like the pages . . . I'm sorry, Miss, but when you bring the waffles, could you—do you have any "lite" syrup? "Lite" syrup. Lo-cal. Lo-cal syrup. No, that's okay. If you don't have "lite," that's fine. Thank you . . . Where was I? Something about the job. Oh, yeah, Carl said I didn't need to decide now, or even right away, whether to give the money back. I could look for a job in the meantime. I could even work at a job while I was writing the book and save some money in case I wanted to give back the advance at some point in the future. And he's right! I don't have to decide today! I can decide when to give the money back *when I want to*!

I AM A GENIUS!

My editor *loves* the book! I haven't talked to her yet, because I stayed out of the house all day yesterday, dreading her call. Talk about paying interest on money you'll probably never borrow! She *loves* it. That was the message on the machine. "Stuart, this is Andrea. I *love* this book! I wouldn't change a word. Call me! And Stuart, tell Joanne that the Higher Power must have put this book in my life!" Isn't that funny?! Isn't she terrific?! And she's not even in one twelve-step program! I mean, she *loves* the book! *Loves* it! How about that, Critical Inner Voice! You're not so smart now, are you? Ha ha! She *loves* the book. I am a genius. And I don't mean that in a grandiose way. We're all geniuses! That's right. Say it. "I am a genius!" You may not believe it right away. You might be saying, "But I'm not even above average." That's okay. You don't have to be above average to be a genius. Everybody's a genius! In their own special way. It may be the way you tie your shoe or . . . I don't know, the way you breathe. Me, I'm a genius because I'm writing a book that my editor *loves!* Ha ha ha ha ha ha!

I AM THE WORLD'S BIGGEST FOOL.

Okay. I just want to kill myself. I spoke to Andrea, and she loves the book all right. And let me tell you why. Evidently, unbeknownst to me, I have been writing, and I quote, "a brilliant *how-not-to* book." My life, it seems, is some kind of humorous textbook example of how *not* to recover from addictive behaviors and attitudes. Why, everyone at Dell is just beside themselves at what a hilariously pathetic life is lived by this "character" I "created." Well, this character just wants to crawl into a hole and never come out. Oh, but that's funny, isn't it? Pathetic Stuart wanting to crawl into a hole. I mean, this is great, isn't it? I can just go on writing about my wretched little life and everybody can just laugh and laugh and laugh. Well, I can't stand it any longer. I'm just turning off the tape recorder. . . . Okay, I've turned it back on, because I want to say just one thing. I'm not giving those bastards the money back! If they want a how-not-to recover daily affirmation book, I'll give it to them!

TODAY I BEGIN ANEW!

called Andrea this morning and told her about how excited I am that she likes my "how-not-to-recover" book. So today I start by *letting go* of yesterday's disappointment, and *beginning anew* with eager anticipation toward my new goal: *intentionally* writing a "how-not-to recover" book. Uh-oh! I find that I am *holding on to* past disappointments! I am not beginning anew! As a result, instead of feeling good about myself, I am feeling bad. I guess by *holding on to* past disappointments, I am demonstrating *how not to* recover. Well, enough for now. I guess I'll just obsess about my past mistakes for the rest of the day!

I HAVE A RIGHT TO MY ANGER!

Carl, my OA sponsor, is worried about me. After reading yesterday's entry, he said he felt it was sarcastic, which is not like me. He said sarcasm was an expression of anger. I said, "No shit, Sherlock!" and hung up. I called him right back and made an immediate amends. But he's right. I am angry! Furious! But that's okay! I am entitled to my anger! I used to be afraid of my anger, because I thought that if I allowed myself to be angry, I would kill someone. Literally. That I would commit a homicide! So I stuffed my anger. And I stuffed my face! Which is why I weighed nearly three hundred pounds. And because I stuffed my anger, it would come out all sideways, in inappropriate ways. Like with sarcasm. Is that how-not-to enough for you, Andrea?

I HAVE BEEN HIT BY A BUS!

What a pathetic wretch am I! When Carl picked me up at the emergency room, I told him he was right: I was angry. But not just angry, I'd been walking around in a rage! All day I kept losing patience with people. If I was in a store and thought someone was standing in a stupid place, blocking the aisle, I'd bump into them. Deliberately. Then later, I was trying to get a cab, and this bus is just sitting there in the middle of the street. Well, I've got all these bags and the taxis can't see me because this bus is in the way. So, of course, I stomp out there ten feet in front of the bus just as it decides to take off. I'm staring at the driver, *daring* him to hit me. And he does. But I don't think he could have stopped. Well, of course, now there's this tremendous scene, and I'm feeling like the incredible jerk I am. These people are standing over me, and yelling at the driver, and I don't have the guts to tell everybody it was my fault. So an ambulance takes me to the emergency room, where I'm told I have a sprained knee and a broken arm. I call Carl, but the first person there to see me was this lawyer, who can't understand why I won't sue the city. Carl arrives, and suggests that I write the Transit Authority and tell them what happened as an amends to the bus driver. Now, this lawyer is still hanging around, and I'm feeling so guilty I tell him what really happened, and he starts yelling at me for wasting his time. This reminds me of Dale, my rage-aholic ex, and by this time my rage is a distant memory, and I'm wishing the bus had killed me. Carl tells me to keep my sense of humor, and my rage comes back for a second; I yell at Carl and then make an immediate amends.

I Am a Fraud! II

I've decided to give the money back. I can't go on with this book. Carl thinks I should probably put off making a decision for at least a week in light of what happened yesterday. He says I'm in a bad frame of mind. But I think I've been putting it off far too long. My editor was right. This is a how-not-to book. How-not-to write a book! Then I told Carl something I am very ashamed of, something I haven't been able to verbalize even to myself. . . . I am—Jesus, I can't say it. C'mon, Stuart, you're only as sick as your secrets. I—I am doing this book under false pretenses! There, I said it! When Dell bought this book, in November, I was on TV with my cable access show, *Daily Affirmations with Stuart Smalley*. I'm sure that's the only reason Dell wanted the book. I was on TV. I mean, why else would they let me do this? I'm not even a licensed therapist. Then in December, my show was moved from twelve noon to 2:45 A.M. by a woman at the cable company, Roz Weinman, who is herself very dysfunctional. I, stupidly, acted out on the air and attacked Roz, and even though I made an immediate amends, she yanked my show off the air. And I didn't tell Dell. I'm sure they think I'm still on the cable somewhere, preaching the gospel of daily affirmations to thousands of insatiable recovery book buyers a day. There you have it. My dirty little secret. This book is one big humongous lie. I'm giving the money back!

TODAY I AM DEPRESSED.

I called Andrea, my editor, and told her I couldn't finish the book and that I was returning the money, or at least for the moment, what's left of it. She told me not to panic, that she loved the pages so far and again she said that it was really a great how-not-to book. I told her it wasn't actually a how-not-to book, and there was a very long pause. Then Andrea said she hoped I understood that she had been laughing *with* me, not *at* me. I lied, and told her that that was my understanding. Then she asked me if I had written anything since then, and I told her yes, and told her about being hit by the bus. Then there was another long pause, after which Andrea suggested that maybe I should go to one of my meetings. But I told her I needed to stay in bed.

THIS TOO SHALL PASS.

The last two weeks have been a living hell. This time I ate Fig Newtons. They don't make as many crumbs as graham crackers, and that can make a difference when you don't change the sheets. Question: How many Fig Newtons can one person eat? Answer: A lot! At first I turned off the phone, but after a few days I turned on the machine to find out who was calling. My sponsors phoned, especially Carl and Fred. Carl came by a couple of times, but I pretended not to be home. But you know who called the most? Andrea, my editor. *"Stuart, this is Andrea. I just wanted to tell you not to worry about the advance. Keep it. You deserve it, honest. Give me a call." "Stuart, this is Andrea. Are you okay?" "Stuart, this is Andrea. I just wanted to tell you I've reread the pages and I think they're great on their own terms. I totally misunderstood them the first time through. I'm sorry. It's terrific, really!" "Stuart, are you there? It's just that I know from your February 17th entry that sometimes you screen your calls. Are you angry with me? I feel really responsible."* Well, yesterday I'm in bed watching an *Oprah* on agoraphobia—perfect—except that none of the agoraphobics showed up, and she's talking to this one *former* agoraphobic who is now a public speaker on agoraphobia. Anyway, the doorbell rings, and I'm thinking, "Okay, Carl's been out here four times now, I really should answer the door." Well, I open it, and I see this woman, this huge woman. And she says, *"Stuart? I'm Andrea."* And I realize that the svelte, sophisticated, urbane voice I heard over the phone from New York weighs nearly three hundred pounds! Andrea had flown a thousand miles just to see if I was okay! And she tells me that this whole episode had made her realize how out of control her own life was and that she had joined OA! Well, I get dressed, and we're off to a meeting. And suddenly, I'm feeling fine!

TODAY I WILL HONOR MY CRITICAL INNER VOICE!

Thank God for Andrea! I never realized how important a good editor can be. After the meeting we went to a coffee shop for fruit salad, salad, and water, and we just talked and talked, until she had to catch her plane back to New York. I just love her! Andrea did ask me not to discuss her life here in the book, and I will, of course, respect that. All I will say is that anyone who thinks there are no Jewish alcoholics should hear about her family of origin! Forgive me, Andrea, and you can take that out if you like. I wouldn't consider it rewriting. Anyway, we talked about why I was having so much trouble writing the book. I mean, Andrea thinks everything I've written so far is great, it's just that I'm having so much trouble emotionally. Now let me tell you, Andrea has been in the program maybe five minutes, but she is incredibly intuitive! And she made me realize something. I got depressed because I had *exhausted* myself *fighting* my Critical Inner Voice! I have been doing *constant* battle with my C.I.V. sapping me until I finally just gave in and said, "Gee, C.I.V., you must be right." Well, doggone it, why do I have to fight it? Why can't I say, "Hey, C.I.V., I hear you. And you are a part of me. I accept you." "Oh, yeah?" says C.I.V. "You don't know what you're talking about, you worthless moron. If you accept me, you're accepting that you're a useless piece of crap." "That's not true," says I. "I can accept that you're there, but not buy into the negative things you say." "You're even crazier than I thought," says C.I.V., "that's the lamest thing I've ever heard." "I knew you'd say that," I say, "but I really think I'm on to something here." "*You* on to something? Don't make me—" "Shuttup!" See? There, I'm fighting it again. I should have just said, "Critical Inner Voice, that's *your* opinion, and I'm going to recognize it as such. But my opinion is different. So if you don't mind, we'll agree to disagree. Oh, and by the way, that 'crap' stuff is inappropriate, and I will not be talked to like that." I can't wait to fax this to Andrea!

TODAY I WILL GET ON WITH MY LIFE!

Andrea loved the dialogue with my Critical Inner Voice. But she says she's still worried about my emotional well-being. She thinks I might be obsessing a little too much about the book. My *editor* thinks I might be obsessing too much about the book! And you know what? She's right! Sometimes in life, we come to realize that by obsessing about something, we give it too much power over us. And sometimes if we just decide to allow ourselves to stop, the thing loses its power. This doesn't always work. I remember when I was living with Dale, the rage-aholic. I wanted to leave, but I just didn't have the courage. I walked around absolutely distraught, angry, overwhelmed by fear and confusion. *I should leave. This person's a rage-aholic. How much yelling can one person take?! But I'll never find anyone else; after all, I weigh nearly three hundred pounds!* Then I went to my first OA meeting, and this woman, I don't remember her name, said that I had the choice to stop obsessing about Dale. I thought she was crazy. And I couldn't stop. Then one day, I was walking past a doughnut shop. Past isn't the right word. I stopped in front of this doughnut shop, and boy did I want a doughnut. But I said, "I have a choice not to eat the doughnut." And I didn't. And that's the moment I stopped obsessing about Dale. I left about a month later. So maybe if I just decide to allow myself to stop obsessing about the book, I will be less afraid of it, and actually write it a lot better. Although Andrea says it's great so far, so maybe I should let well enough alone and keep obsessing. No, but Andrea thinks that it would healthier for me to stop obsessing, and of course, she's right. . . . You know, now that I think back to that moment when I chose not to eat that doughnut, I remember that I had just eaten a huge pizza. I wonder if that had anything to do with it. Probably doesn't matter. I think I'll type this up, fax it to Andrea, and then give her a ring to see what she thinks.

TODAY I WILL GET ON WITH MY LIFE! II

Andrea thinks I may be developing an unhealthy codependent relationship with her. Of course, she's right. I can't believe I do this to myself. I mean, who would have thought it, Stuart Smalley using his editor as a crutch? *Quel* surprise! Anyway, Andrea thinks it's probably a bad idea for me to fax her every day. She put it very nicely and made a good point. She says I had been doing fine by myself, at least with the writing, and that she would be enabling me if I depended on her response to every day's affirmation. I can't believe how direct and yet compassionate she was. And she's only been in the program for like seventy-two hours! I suggested I fax her every *other* day, and she suggested once a week. So we compromised at twice a week, which really is every three days. So . . . I'll just have to wait a couple days before sending this off. I hope it's good. Anyway, in the meantime, I've just got to get on with my life!

I WILL USE THE PHONE!

In twelve-step programs we have a slogan, "Use the Phone." Too often when something is bothering us, we isolate (don't I know!) instead of picking up the phone and talking to someone. Not a well-meaning friend or family member, but someone who really knows and understands what we're going through. Someone in the program. Anyway, the whole thing with Andrea had me kind of upset last night, so I called someone in the program. Andrea. Which was stupid. I forgot the hour time difference in New York, so I guess it was kind of late when I got her. In fact, I think I woke her up, because she seemed confused. For the first twenty seconds or so, she didn't know what day it was. I apologized and offered to call her at her office in the morning, but by then she was awake and insisted on hearing what was troubling me. So I told her and then asked her if it was okay if I could talk to her more often than once every three days if it wasn't about the book and it wasn't in the middle of the night. There was a long pause, and then she said it was all right for now, but that we had to be careful that our personal relationship didn't interfere with our professional relationship. Then, for some God knows what reason, I offered to be her OA sponsor. There was another long pause, which I could not stand and interrupted by saying, "Sorry, that was really dumb and inappropriate," and she sounded very relieved that I said that. At this point I was feeling like a giant fool, and I wanted to say just the right thing, but of course, instead I said the exact wrong thing, which was to talk about the book. There was still another pause, during which I was dying, and then Andrea said that she thought I still might be obsessing too much about the book and maybe I was developing this codependent attachment to her because she's the editor of the book. And that's when she suggested I get a job. At this point I start to freak out. While she's saying, "Stuart, having all day to obsess about this book is just not healthy," I'm thinking, "She's telling me the book is no good and I have to return the money, and that's why she's telling me to get a job." Which, of course, is Stinkin' Thinkin', which I've been doing a lot of lately. By now I am not even hearing what she is saying, and I have this knot in the pit of my stomach, and I'm thinking I'm going to take to my bed for another month.

I AM A VALUABLE EMPLOYEE!

When I described the Andrea phone call to Ray, my Al-Anon sponsor, he said I needed a meeting. I hit the twelve noon at the Unitarian church and got my good hand up and shared about the call. About halfway through, Ray started to laugh, then Bonnie, then Tina, and by the end, everyone in the room was howling, including me! Well, the rest of the meeting became this orgy of codependent phone call stories. For some reason my favorite was Michael's. He and his wife are in the middle of a trial separation, and she's living in Milwaukee. So one night last week he feels compelled to call her, and when she asks why, he says it was to remind her to use their SPRINT number! Well, the meeting just lifted this enormous ten-ton weight, and I realized that Andrea was right. I just have too much time on my hands to obsess about the book. *I'm going to get a job!* And when I look for employment, I have to remember that *I am a valuable employee!* I should be, I'm a codependent! In fact, I think I'll put that on my résumé. "Codependent—1951 to present. Will work too hard, be overresponsible, and you can pay me nothing. I'll resent you for it. But that's okay. I'll be too scared to say anything." You know, it's tempting. I'd either get an employer with a sense of humor or some twisted sicko like my last boss. Well, doggone it, this time I *refuse* to work in a dysfunctional environment! Well, anyway, a *severely* dysfunctional environment. I'm too valuable for that!

FIRST THINGS FIRST!

I'm already benefiting from my decision to get a job. I find I'm a lot less worried about this book, since I've started obsessing about writing my résumé. Oh, yesterday I faxed Andrea the last three days' affirmations, and she thought they were terrific. She just thought that maybe I should include less about her and our relationship in the book itself, and I think that's fair. So that's all I'll say about that. . . . Except to say that she's really terrific and I really respect the way she's handling this. Anyway. I am scared to death about writing this résumé. I mean, I've been writing this book every day for two and a half months (minus the month and a half I was in bed). But I haven't written a résumé in years. My last civilian, i.e., *non-recovery*, job was in, get this, public relations. I know. But believe me, when it comes to touting *other* people's abilities, I'm great. Gee, I wonder if you're supposed to put on the résumé why you left your last job? I was fired. Or I quit, I'm not sure. It was the day after the Persian Gulf War started. Our firm represented a company that made wheelchairs, and of course, who do you think was assigned to the account? Well, the night we started bombing Iraq, my boss tells me to pitch all the financial papers and magazines the next morning. I was supposed to tell these financial editors, "Gee, a lot of our boys are going to come back maimed, and they're going to need wheelchairs, aren't they? Don't you think your readers should get in on the profits?" Well, I slept on it, and the next morning I told my boss that I thought that strategy might backfire, people might think taking advantage of other people's suffering was in bad taste. I can't remember exactly what my boss said, but I'm sure the words "fat" and "idiot" were in there somewhere. Then I either quit or was fired. Maybe I should just save this for the interview. Right now, it's first things first, and I gotta write this résumé!

FIRST THINGS FIRST! II

Okay. I went out and got a book on writing résumés. And the book suggested that before I write the résumé, I think about who I will be submitting the résumé to. Pretty obvious, but I didn't think of it. But that's okay! I went out and got a book, and the book told me what to do. Okay. Where do I want to work? Do I want to work at another public relations firm? I don't know. But that's okay. I don't have to know. Okay. Wait a minute. I just glanced at the book and the book says I should decide what my "professional objectives" are before I decide where to work. Okay. So that comes first. That's pretty obvious too. But that's okay. I'm sorry, you already know it's okay. Okay. I think what's wrong here is that I've been skipping around in the book. I didn't read the introduction first. Which is okay. I really should read the introduction first, but I shouldn't beat myself up for not. Okay. First things first. I'm going to read the introduction!

I CAN SET MY OWN GOALS!

All my life I've let other people set my goals for me. Some-times I think the goals were set up for me to fail. My Dad wanted me to be a big football jock, so I tried out for the team when I was in sixth grade. The coach put me on the line be-cause I weighed nearly two hundred pounds, but my heart just wasn't in it. I thought it was a stupid game, and I guess I just didn't have the killer instinct. Although once in a scrimmage, on a really muddy day, Brad Ralles called me a fat sissy. On the next play, about six guys tackled him and as Brad went down, I could see his face sink into the mud with all those guys on top of him. I took a flying leap and landed on top as hard as I could, pushing the pile down another six inches. The other guys started yelling for me to get off, because they could hear Brad's muffled screams. But I just lay there, and since I outweighed everyone by about a hundred pounds, it wasn't until the coach dragged me off that the other guys could jump up. The coach pulled Brad out, and he was okay after coughing up about a ton of mud. So when I say I used to be afraid of allowing myself to be angry because I thought I might kill someone, you can see what I mean! Anyway, I was kicked off the team for almost suffocating Brad, and he tormented me all the way through the twelfth grade, as did my Dad. So, cut to 1989, my twentieth high school reunion, which I decided to go to because I had lost about eighty pounds. Who's there but Brad Ralles. I decide to make an amends to him and guess what? He's six years in AA, and in two minutes we're crying and hugging. Okay . . . I just have no idea where I am.

I WILL LOVE MY INNER CHILD!

I faxed Andrea the last three affirmations, and she flipped over yesterday's Brad Ralles story! "More inner child! Give me more inner child!" (I think she just read some Bradshaw!) Anyway, when people talk about the *inner child* they're talking about the little boy or girl we were when we were growing up in our dysfunctional family. (I heard in a meeting that 96 percent of all families are dysfunctional, which if you ask me, means that people who grew up in functional families are pretty darn weird!) Anyway, in a dysfunctional family that little boy or girl doesn't get the kind of love and nurturing he or she needs. And the child adapts to this unhealthy, dysfunctional situation by pretending that he doesn't need the parenting and becomes an adultified survivor. But that little child still exists in all of us. . . . I'm sorry, I'm getting upset. Okay, Stuart, pull yourself together. Okay. Anyway, this little child still exists in all adults. In a way, it's really the spiritual part of us. I guess. I just thought of that. Anyway, *loving* the inner child is really about reparenting the little boy or girl that didn't get what they needed the first time 'round. And that means *listening.* So in deciding my employment goals, *I will listen to my inner child!*

I WILL DRIVE AN ICE CREAM TRUCK IN TAHITI!

Go ahead. *You* tell my inner child that's unrealistic!

TODAY I WILL LAUGH—AT LEAST ONCE!

You know what? So far yesterday's affirmation is my favorite! Oh, I know it's stupid. But that's why I like it! I made myself laugh! Sometimes things seem so bleak that it's hard for us to see the humor in life. I don't think I laughed once from 1984 to 1987, my last four years with Dale, the rage-aholic. But laughter is such a great release! It's like the mind and the soul having sex! Not with each other . . . Anyway, it's a release. And laughter can help us put things in their true perspective. Like my "professional objectives," which the résumé book suggested I decide on before I write my résumé. Yesterday's joke, which made me laugh, also made me realize something. *This* is my professional objective! Helping people by sharing my experience, strength, and hope in this book of daily affirmations. The reason I'm getting a job is to give me something else to focus on so I don't drive myself crazy. So, as far as this job search goes, I have no professional objectives! It took me four days and a really lame joke to figure that out. But that's okay!

I DESERVE GOOD THINGS!

"I'm wearing a cardboard belt!" Zero Mostel exclaimed in one of my favorite movies, *The Producers*. Mostel played a Broadway producer down on his luck who was pointing out how broke he was. Pretty pathetic, huh? Well, *I've* worn a cardboard belt when I had money in the bank! Why? Because I didn't think I was entitled to a leather one. When I was dieting, I'd figure I might as well wait until I got down to "my Viet Cong weight." (The ideal weight for an American male my height—five-foot-eight—is 155 pounds. The last time I weighed 155, I was ten. But that was never a good enough goal for me. Until recovery my goal my entire adult life has been to weigh what the average five-foot-eight Viet Cong weighed during the Tet offensive!) Anyway, when I was losing weight, I would put off buying the leather belt, and when I was gaining weight, well, cardboard was almost too good for pond scum like me! So when I look for this job, I have to remember, I deserve good things! I deserve a good salary! *I deserve a leather belt!* Okay. I just thought of something. For any . . . oh, vegetarian, anti-fur, pro-cow people, just make it, "I deserve a well-made canvas belt" . . . or something, I don't know.

TODAY I WILL PUT THE FOCUS ON ME!

All too often, we forget that we alone are responsible for our happiness. That no matter what is happening around us, we can choose whether or not to be happy. "There are no victims, only volunteers," as we say in Al-Anon. Take for example, Joanne, whom you may remember as my Debtors Anonymous friend who believes the Higher Power put a parking spot in her life. Well, I thought she would like yesterday's affirmation, since getting paid what you deserve is a big DA issue. So I got Joanne at work, and she was crying. She's been in this relationship for six months now, and her boyfriend just cannot commit. We ended up talking for hours. I had planned to write my résumé, but she was very upset and needed to talk. I can't go into the whole thing, but suffice it to say her boyfriend has difficulty with intimacy issues and has been acting very distant. If Joanne says "I love you," he doesn't say it right back, whereas two months ago he did. That sort of thing. But I don't want to go into the whole story, because it's very involved. Anyway, I told her to keep the focus on herself. Like I do. Well, she called me back in the evening, and thanked me, and said that her Higher Power had put my phone call in her life. Which made me feel terrific!

JOANNE HAS BROKEN UP WITH HER BOYFRIEND!

Andrea, my editor, loved the ice cream truck joke, and thinks things are going great, but she was a little concerned that I haven't gotten to my résumé in over a week. Well, I was actually sitting down at the typewriter when Joanne called, and believe me, this was a crisis! I don't want to get into the whole thing. Suffice it to say that she discovered that her boyfriend, whom I will call Bob, because . . . okay, well, that's his name. Anyway, Bob had dinner with his old girlfriend. And suffice it to say, Bob's best friend, whom I will call . . . Dr. X . . . told Joanne that he believes that Bob is still in love with his old girlfriend, whose name I do not know. But it's more complicated than that. I just don't have enough room to get into it. Anyway, Joanne called Bob and told him off and told him that he is emotionally a child, not in the inner-child sense but in the bad way, and that he had difficulty with intimacy issues, which is what I told her, and that she never wants to see him again. So you can see why I didn't get to my résumé today.

TODAY I WILL STAY AWAY FROM SICK, TWISTED PEOPLE!

Okay. It turns out that Dr. X, Joanne's boyfriend's "best friend," is a very unhealthy person with his own sick agenda—getting into Joanne's pants! Which in and of itself is not sick. Joanne is a very attractive woman. She's a dancer, and believe me, her legs go on forever. And sex is a wonderful, joyful gift that God gave us and that we should enjoy, if we can do it without exploiting other people. And that is just what was happening in this thing with Joanne and Dr. X, who by the way is *not* a doctor, so from now on, I'll call him Ted. Anyway, as you remember, Ted told Joanne that Bob had dinner with his old girlfriend, whose name I do not know, but will call Theresa, and that Bob still loves Theresa. So Joanne called Bob, told him off, and ended their relationship. So yesterday, Ted suggests that he and Joanne go out to dinner to . . . you know, discuss Bob. Yeah, right! Well, after dinner, Ted invites Joanne up to his place, and Joanne says no, she has to get up early for work, so he offers to walk her home, and of course, asks to come in to make a phone call. And that's where he hits on her. Well, to the guy's credit he took no for an answer, but this put everything he said about Bob and Theresa in a slightly different light, to say the least! So Joanne kicks the guy out, and calls Bob, who's not home. So she calls me. And I tell her again, "Keep the focus on yourself!"

I AM AN HONEST PERSON. II

I called Joanne this morning to see how she was holding up, and Bob answered. I didn't want to complicate things by making him jealous, so I panicked and lied and said I was a gay male dancer friend of hers. And he believed it! Joanne got on, and I told her I had lied, and she said that it was okay and that I should call her at the office. I felt so bad about lying that I called Ray, my Al-Anon sponsor, who suggested I get to a meeting. At the meeting I shared about lying, and about how much trouble I was having with my résumé. After the meeting I went out to coffee with Michael, the guy who's separated from his wife. He told me that he thought maybe I wasn't being honest *with myself*. That maybe I had invested so much time and effort in Joanne's drama because I didn't want to work on my résumé. Well, I got right home and started working on it, when, of course, Joanne phoned, wondering why I hadn't called her at the office. I decided to be totally honest, and I told her what Michael had said. And then she said the oddest thing. She said she didn't know I was looking for a job. I guess all the times I had talked to her, I hadn't said a thing about myself! She felt terrible, but I told her it was my fault. I was the one who hadn't been honest with me!

FIRST THINGS FIRST! III

Okay. This is very strange. I have a job interview. Arranged by Joanne. With Ted, her boyfriend, Bob's, best friend, who hit on her. I had considered him a sick, twisted person, but he owns a small PR firm, and is looking for a new assistant. I told Joanne that no way was I going to work for another sicko, but then Joanne told me that maybe Ted wasn't really so bad. Evidently, Ted had been telling the truth. Bob *had* gone to dinner with his old girlfriend Theresa, and he *had* told Ted that he still thought he loved her. According to Joanne, Bob told her that he went to dinner with Theresa with the purpose of telling her that he couldn't talk to her on the phone anymore, because he felt he was deceiving Joanne, whom he really does love and thought that the phone calls were making it impossible for him emotionally to make a commitment. But Ted didn't know that part of it, which Bob has corroborated to Joanne, although Joanne has not told Bob that Ted hit on her. Joanne feels that Ted was acting out of genuine concern for her, and when he hit on her, she might have kind of encouraged it in a way by saying at dinner that he was an extremely attractive man, which she might have done because she was angry at Bob. I know this sounds complicated, but if I'm going to try to get this job, it's important for me to know that Ted is not a slimeball. Anyway, this seems like the perfect job for me right now, but I want to make sure I'm not going to jump in just as an excuse to avoid writing my résumé. So first things first! Today I will write my résumé!

TODAY I WILL SET CLEAR AND DISTINCT BOUNDARIES, WHICH OTHERS CANNOT CROSS!

Tomorrow is my interview with Ted. I'm overqualified for the job, personal assistant to the head of a small PR firm. After all, I was a press agent myself. But right now I just don't need that kind of responsibility. After all, I have this book to write! Not that being a personal assistant is easy, because let me tell you, if you don't set boundaries right away, you become a slave. I know, because I've also been a slave. Too many times. For my bosses, for my parents, for Dale. But this is about work, so I'll keep today's affirmation about setting boundaries at work. I used to be available to my employer twenty-four hours a day. Got a problem at three in the morning? Call Stuart. Wake up Stuart's roommate! Cause Stuart's roommate to scream at Stuart. Oh God, that was hell! Once I got a call from my boss at two in the morning. He was in France and had lost his passport. I had to get him a replacement by the next day, because he was flying to Italy. So now it's two-fifteen in the morning and I'm calling this friend of mine who's a slave in our senator's home office, who calls this woman who's a slave at the passport office. And, of course, the slave network works its magic and gets my boss the passport in time for his flight. Well, pretty soon, I'm getting passports at a moment's notice for my boss's clients, for his clients' friends, et cetera, et cetera, ad infinitum. And why? Because I set no boundaries. Well, tomorrow I will be polite, I will be nice, I will share myself as a loving human being on this planet, but *I will establish boundaries!*

I'M GOOD ENOUGH, I'M SMART ENOUGH, AND DOGGONE IT, PEOPLE LIKE ME!

Okay. My job interview is in an hour. I am very nervous, but that's okay! I am entitled to be nervous! I don't know why I'm nervous. I'm not sure I even want this job. I am not sure I approve of this employer, Ted, who hit on Joanne, although it may have been her fault to some extent, and he may have been . . . I'm sorry, okay. I'm very nervous. But that's okay! Okay. It's hard for me to concentrate on today's affirmation, because I am so nervous. But I just have to remember I am a valuable employee! I can think of creative solutions to difficult problems! I believe in me! I'm good enough! I'm smart enough! And doggone it, people like me! And even if I don't believe it, it's because I'm being told otherwise by my Critical Inner Voice, which I should honor and not fight. And I have to remember to set boundaries. Okay. I'm beginning to feel overwhelmed. I should just love my inner child and remember that I deserve good things. Wish me luck!

I REFUSE TO BEAT MYSELF UP!

I sucked so bad in that interview! I tried to be smart; I tried to be funny; and I just made a giant, humongous fool of myself! But that's okay! I'm not perfect! I'm a human being. Human beings make mistakes! Wow! Was I bad! I interrupted the man. I tried to impress him with how much I know about the business. I was incredibly transparent, flattering the man, telling him how excited I'd be to work there. And setting boundaries? I offered to bring in my own espresso machine so he could have decaf cappuccinos in the afternoon! There must be something desperately wrong with me. Okay. That's just Stinkin' Thinkin', and I refuse to beat myself up! I know he's just going to call Joanne and tell her what a flake her friend is. But that's okay. Joanne knows me from the program and loves me unconditionally. Thank God! I'm just sorry I let her down. I'm supposed to find out sometime today. God, it's a nightmare! . . . Excuse me, Miss, do you have any lo-cal syrup? Lo-cal. Low calorie. Diet syrup.

I HAVE A RIGHT TO MY ANGER!

When I got home last night, the flashing light on the message machine indicated that I had one message. This is it, I thought. Ted's six-months-pregnant assistant calling to say I didn't get the job, that they were interested in someone a little less emotionally crippled. Well, the call turned out to be from Andrea, my editor, who said she was just checking in to see how I was doing, because she hadn't heard from me in a week. Which meant that Ted's office did not call, which is very dysfunctional and abusive, because he told me I'd hear by the end of the day. So, of course, by this time, I am now very angry. Which is okay; I am entitled to my anger! So I call Andrea at home and offer to read her the last seven affirmations, and she says that's okay, it can wait till the morning. And I tell her, no, that's okay, I'd like to read them now. So I read them and ask for her reaction, and she says she'd like to wait till the morning when she can really sit down and read them. Which is when I start yelling at her. I mean, she calls me, complains about not hearing from me in a week, and then hates what I've written. She just tells me she's sorry I feel that way, but she has to get back to her dinner guests. Of course, five minutes later, I realize what I've done, and call Andrea and make an amends. And I realize I shouldn't be angry at all. If the place is that dysfunctional, I should be glad I didn't get the job. I should be grateful.

I GOT THE JOB!

know you're thinking, April Fool! But no. Joanne called this morning, after she got home from Bob's. There was a message on her machine from Ted, who told her I got the job, but that the phone number I had given his assistant was wrong. For some God-knows-what reason I had written my number down wrong! And my phone's not listed, because immediately after I left our abusive relationship, Dale, the rage-aholic, would call me at all hours and scream at me. I start tomorrow!

MY AUNT PAULA DIED.

I t's not tomorrow yet. I have to write two entries today, and I know it's the worst day to do that because it must seem like an April Fools joke. But it's not. Honest. My Aunt Paula died. My sister, Jodie, called just as I finished my last affirmation. And I'm flying home tomorrow. Ted understands and told me to stay in Minnesota as long as I have to. I think he's going to be a great boss! Aunt Paula was my great-aunt and she was ninety-two, which means she outlived every one of her brothers and sisters by about thirty years. I think that's because she was the only one who didn't drink. There's lots of ways to die from alcoholism. Liver disease, car accidents, sure. But three Smalley men have met their Maker falling off the roof while cleaning leaves out of the gutters. Well, that's not true. Uncle Pete got smashed one Sunday afternoon, climbed up on the roof to trim the big elm, and cut through a power line with the shears. The doctor said he was dead well before he hit the ground. I loved Aunt Paula. She was an old maid, so she helped take care of me and my brother and my sister. I'd lay across her lap and she would tickle my back while I watched TV, and I'd get goose bumps. Since I've been an adult, she was really the only one who would talk to me about our family history. Her brother, Stuart, my Dad's dad, my grandfather and namesake, was an alcoholic, never really held down a job, and died at about fifty, about a week before I was born. I never knew him or my grandmother. She raised eight kids, and according to Aunt Paula, usually had two jobs, one as a scrubwoman and the other taking in laundry, and she died when she was forty-seven. Aunt Paula said it was from "exhaustion."

I WILL TRACE IT, FACE IT, AND ERASE IT!

My brother, Donnie, picked me up at the airport with his motorcycle. My sister, Jodie, was supposed to pick me up, but she's going through an ugly divorce and her husband slashed the tires on her car while it was parked in front of the funeral home and Donnie filled in at the last minute because Mom was cooking for the wake, and Dad won't let anyone drive his car, and no one wanted to let him pick me up. So Donnie let me use his helmet and lashed my bags to the chopper with bungee cords. Ah! Home! Trace it, face it, and erase it! I heard that in an Al-Anon room once. And as I held on to my older brother for dear life, bombing through the streets of south Minneapolis on the way to see the cadaver of the only adult who gave a damn about me when I was a kid, I vowed that this trip I would dispassionately observe where I came from, process it, and then spit it out behind me! But now it's the next morning, and I'm here in the room where I grew up, dictating into my tape recorder, and I feel so sad. And the crazy part is, I want to step in and save these people. Is that sick or what?

I AM NOT MY PARENTS!

I forgot how much I hate my parents. You'd think that would be something you remember. It must be like labor. They say women forget the pain of giving birth, because otherwise they wouldn't have any more children. We forget the pain of visiting home, because otherwise we'd never come back. And I'll tell you, this has been worse than shitting a watermelon, excuse the French. Where do I begin? Dad spends most of his time in the garage where he can "putter," code word for getting loaded, and, of course, avoid Mom. And who wouldn't? She's been cooking up a storm for the wake. One look at Mom and you know that food is everything to this woman. I mean, when I was a kid, me and Mom and Jodie would play pick-up sticks with French fries! Not really. It's just a joke I tell in OA. Anyway, she's made a glazed ham for the wake, because glazed ham is what the Smalleys have at wakes. Every family event has its own special foods. Thanksgiving is turkey with giblet dressing, Christmas is turkey with bread stuffing, christenings are roast beef and French fries. We play pick-up sticks at christenings! I am not lying! Jodie made a glazed ham for her son's christening and Mom made her throw it out—it was bad luck. Glazed hams are for wakes! At least in the Smalley family. And Mom has enshrined in her mind all our incredibly joyful family gatherings with these wonderful remembrances of foods past. (Remember that glazed ham I made for Uncle Pete's wake?) So, of course, the fact that I'm in OA is very threatening to her, even though she pretends to be all in favor of it. "It's just too bad that these things don't seem to work over the long haul." At least Dad is openly hostile. When he said he told me that my cable access show would be canceled, I had to admit he was right. Then I told him and Mom about the book, and Mom said she hoped I wouldn't fall off the OA wagon when the book wasn't published, and I said that actually the book was going well, and that it was turning out kind of autobiographical. At which point Dad said, "What's it called? *Waste of Space?* And then I remembered that when I was growing up, Dad always used to say that I took up too much space. I got upset and went into the living room, where Donnie was watching two-man volleyball on ESPN and smoking pot. I told him what happened, and he got p.o.'d and walked into the kitchen and said, "Hey, Dad, whattaya say me and Stuart help you change the storm windows? You know, crack a coupla cool ones, get on the roof. Could be fun!" Thank God the funeral is today!

I REFUSE TO LIVE FROM CRISIS TO CRISIS! II

Okay. I have to stay at least another day. Because we couldn't bury Aunt Paula. We tried. But the police stopped us. Actually, it was my cousins. Okay. Let me back up. About ten yesterday morning, we got a call from the director of the funeral house. Evidently, my cousins, the Von Arks, who are Aunt Paula's sister's kids, my Dad's first cousins, and who are estranged from our part of the family (Gee, I don't know why!), had seen Aunt Paula's death listed in the paper, and then snooped around at the cemetery and realized we were going to lay Aunt Paula to rest in the family plot. Anyway, supposedly there were sixteen places in the plot and two were still vacant. But it turns out *fifteen* people are buried in the family plot, not *fourteen*, and everyone suspects that the Von Arks snuck somebody in while we weren't looking. So the Von Arks claim that the one remaining plot is for their father, William, whom they've put in some terrible nursing home. Well, my Dad tells the funeral director to ignore the Von Arks, that Aunt Paula *paid* for the plot herself with her veteran benefits. (She was a WAC during World War II.) Which is true, except that evidently she didn't put her own name on the deed or document or whatever. So we go to church, have the service, follow the hearse to the cemetery and there are the police and the Von Arks. So here we are over the graves of fifteen blood relatives, or fourteen, depending on who's in there, and of course every bit of family history gets dredged up, who didn't who help who when whoever's father died. Poor Aunt Paula would be turning in her grave, if she wasn't in the back of the hearse. And that's when Dad hits the cop. Now I know you're thinking, poor Stuart, but actually, this had been the best part of the trip. Nothing like a crisis and a common enemy to bring the Smalley family together! I mean, our juices were really flowing! The problem starts when Dad and Donnie are being put in the back of the squad car, and Dad tells Mom to cancel the wake. Well . . . you can imagine. "You can't cancel the wake! I made a glazed ham!" "But my Aunt Paula isn't in the ground yet!" "Your Aunt Paula! When did you ever give a damn about your Aunt Paula?" So as far as Mom was concerned, the wake was on, and as far as Dad was concerned, it was canceled. And the rest of us had to choose. Donnie decided to stay in jail with Dad, who refused to be bailed out. Jodie and I went back to the house and helped host the wake. But I was really sad and really mad. Because now the wake was not about Aunt Paula, it was about choosing between Mom and Dad.

I AM AT ONE WITH THE UNIVERSE.

We laid Aunt Paula to rest in a Lutheran cemetery even though she was Presbyterian. But I don't think that meant she was any farther from her Higher Power. Dad and Donnie were released in time for the ceremony, and to say it was uncomfortable would be a slight understatement! Dad just glared at Mom throughout the whole thing. And Donnie was in a bad mood because he hadn't smoked any pot and had just spent an entire night in a cell with Dad, who hadn't had anything to drink. But as I watched them lower Aunt Paula, Dad and Donnie and Mom kind of disappeared. I started to cry and get goose bumps like when Aunt Paula would tickle my back when I'd lay across her lap and watch the *Dick Van Dyke Show* with her. That's when Jodie took my hand. I looked at her and she was crying, too, but she smiled at me. Jodie was holding the hand of her little boy, Kyle, whose dad had slashed his mom's tires and who had just the day before watched his grandpa slug a cop. But for some reason I felt okay. And I squeezed my little sister's hand and said good-bye to my Aunt Paula.

I CAN TAKE A DAY OFF!

I flew back home immediately after the funeral, almost as anxious to get to my new job as I was to get away from Mom and Dad. I had intended to go into work today, but I have to tell you, *I have an emotional hangover!* And you know what, I don't want to think about it, I don't want to talk about it. I'm taking a day off!

MY HIGHER POWER WILL KEEP ME SAFE!

Today is the first day of my new job. In the past I have approached this day with fear, dread, and overwhelming nausea. But today, thanks to the program, the nausea has been replaced by shortness of breath! But that's okay! Progress, not perfection! At least now I can name what's going on. Basically, I am afraid that my new employer will discover that I am no good, fire me, and take out an ad in the paper saying never hire this person, he is a fraud. Then, thanks to recovery, I recognize that that is my Critical Inner Voice talking. And I answer with this affirmation: "I am good enough! I trust in my Higher Power that He will keep me safe and employed! And I've never in my life seen an ad in the paper saying don't hire this person; how likely is it that I'd be the first one?" So, I take a deep breath, let it out, take in another. Wish me luck!

I HAVE MADE TREMENDOUS PROGRESS!

Sometimes I forget to congratulate myself on just how far I've come! Guess what? Yesterday was not a horror! Ted is just terrific. It is so nice to know that I can finally choose to put healthy people in my life! I mean, my last boss would never have let me go home for the funeral. And Ted said he understood the emotional stress of a death in the family and told me to go home early. And you know what? I didn't want to go. His assistant, Marilee, who is breaking me in, is seven months pregnant, and just glowing! A beautiful girl! And she just loves Ted. And why not? He is very distinguished. I'd say fiftyish. And very charming! And sensitive! He took me aside today and told me how much he cares about Joanne, and hopes that she and Bob can stay together, even though he thinks Bob has some real fear of intimacy. And then he reminded me that we had never discussed salary, and he suggested that *I* come up with a figure! I said I'd sleep on it, which is very healthy. I used to think I had to answer right away. He said to remember that I was very valuable and deserved good things. At which point I asked him if he was in DA, Debtors Anonymous, because that's such a big DA issue. But he said he wasn't, and I was tempted to tell him that Joanne was, but it's an anonymous program. Anyway, as Joanne would say, Thank you, Higher Power, for putting this great boss in my life!

I DON'T HAVE TO DO TOO MUCH!

I've decided to ask for three fifths of whatever Marilee makes. She's been Ted's assistant for three years, so I would never ask for more than three fourths of what she gets. She really knows the job and is just terrific. And what a beautiful girl! Also, she does some things for Ted that I am not sure I'm going to do. For example, she travels with him. I discussed this with Ted, and I really want to have the option of staying home and working on the book. So that made me think I should ask for five eighths of Marilee's salary. But then I said to myself, "I am a valuable person!" and realized I should get two thirds of what she makes. But then I started thinking, what if one day I want to go to a meeting? Or just take a walk in the park and smell the flowers! If I take two thirds I may not feel that I can do that. Because sometimes when I take a job, I feel like I have to do everything. And I don't! So three fifths it is!

THERE BUT FOR THE GRACE OF GOD GO I!

Ted insisted that I should get two thirds of whatever it is that Marilee makes, but I held my ground, and took three fifths. I told him I wanted the freedom to bug out if I absolutely needed to, and he joked around and said I can't use an excuse like my Aunt Paula died, because I've already used that one. I think it's so great that in recovery I can laugh at things like that! Ted suggested that it might be fun if he took me and Joanne and Bob to dinner as kind of a celebration of him getting this great new assistant! Oh, one other thing. Marilee is guiding me through the Rolodex. You know, who's important, whose call to put through immediately, and I noticed a woman with Ted's last name. Turns out that Ted is married with two little kids and is going through a very nasty divorce. Marilee says his wife is crazy, and is putting him through hell, trying to prevent him from seeing the kids. Wow! You know, sometimes I sit around feeling sorry for myself, and here some great guy like Ted is going through this hell! And you'd never know it. I mean, here he was joking around to make *me* feel comfortable. Kind of puts you to shame!

I WILL BLESS THOSE AROUND ME WITH LOVE!

I'm beginning to get an idea just how mammoth this job is. Marilee answers the phone, types, does Ted's schedule, his mail, makes lunch and dinner reservations, buys gifts for clients, pops his popcorn, and God knows what else! I think her hardest job is deciding who has access to Ted, since he's so busy. He's not just a press agent himself, but has four agents working for him. One of them, Julia, who handles our biggest account, Pfeiffer, Holden, and Jeffreys, a financial brokerage firm, just hates me. Marilee says Julia is just a very angry person, and I did see her yell yesterday when Marilee wouldn't let her in to see Ted. And the woman will not look at me, let alone talk to me. Marilee thinks Julia doesn't like me because Julia wanted Sandy, the receptionist who's been there two years, to have my job. That makes sense, because Sandy has been kind of weird to me, leaving me on hold a lot when she transfers calls, that kind of thing. So I have decided that *love* is the most powerful tool I can use in this situation, and I will project it onto others! For example, Julia came by on the way to the espresso machine, and I told her how pretty she looked in her new suit, and she is a very pretty girl, sort of an Italian Julia Roberts, only short, with a lovely little petite figure. She kind of rolled her eyes and said a grudging thank you under her breath. But I think it's a start! Oh, one other thing. I made dinner reservations for tonight at Ted's favorite French restaurant, Le Veau d'Or. Unfortunately, Bob's out of town and can't make it, so I guess that just means the three of us, Joanne, me, and Ted, will be discussing Bob!

I AM FUN TO BE WITH!

Sometimes I forget to remind myself that I am a good conversationalist, that I am good company, that I am fun to be with! I think Joanne and Ted got a little looped, which used to make me feel uncomfortable, being an adult child of an alcoholic. But some people can drink and enjoy themselves. And that's okay! It's more than okay! It's absolutely appropriate. Joanne was radiant, and having more fun than I've seen her have in a long time. Of course, I really only mainly see her in DA meetings. Or in the coffee shop afterwards. Anyway, did we have fun! I cannot believe this guy is my boss. Ted was funny; he was charming; and best of all (for a codependent like me), he was singing my praises! In fact, and here's the amazing thing, in the middle of dinner—and I have to tell you, this place is incredible, and so are the prices! But it's worth it, if you have the money. Which Ted does. Anyway, in the middle of dinner, the waiter comes over to the table and hands Ted the phone. It's Marilee. There is this crisis involving Pfeiffer, Holden, and Jeffreys, and Julia wants to see him immediately at the office. Well, guess what? He sends me! Can you believe it! One week at work and he's already using me in a pinch.

I WILL NOT BE JUDGMENTAL OF OTHERS!

Pfeiffer, Holden, and Jeffreys is a regional financial services corporation located here in town. Apparently, a number of PH&J brokers had been involved in a kiting scheme to defraud their clients—mainly small investors—you know, widows and orphans. Well, not orphans. They don't invest. Anyway, an indictment would be coming down next week. (Sorry if this doesn't seem like an entry in the normal daily affirmation book, but I'm doing my best, and that's okay!) Anyway, when Julia explained this whole thing to me, my initial reaction was, "these people are low-life scum." Julia, who was livid that I was there in the first place, said, "Well, they're *our* low-life scum," and told me to leave. But I said my orders from Ted were to write a memo explaining the situation and Julia's recommendations and have it on his desk for the morning. It was getting late, and my "bless those around me with love" affirmation was not working, at least in the form I was trying it, which was to make her cappuccino, act deferential, and tell her how much Ted trusts her judgment. And then I realized, maybe I wasn't really being loving, maybe what had started out as an affirmation had become a *tactic*. I mean, after all, how loving is it to call fellow human beings "low-life scum"? I mean, who am I to judge? Sure, what they did was wrong, but who knows why they felt they had to do it, other than just sheer greed. And maybe greed is just a symptom. What weirdness did they come from, what kind of dysfunction were they exposed to? Aren't they somebody's husband, or daughter, or dad? Julia just looked at me like I was from outer space.

I Am a Catalyst!

At the staff meeting Ted thought my take on the Pfeiffer, Holden, and Jeffreys crisis was "very compassionate." Scott, one of our press agents, thought so, too, but said that trying to win sympathy for these crooked brokers might backfire. What about the husbands, daughters, and dads they stole money from? Then Julia had a breakthrough! She said, "Who are the *real* victims here? I mean, other than the people who had their money stolen? The real victims are the vast majority of *honest*, hardworking PH&J brokers. Husbands, daughters, dads who never in a million years would do anything to breach their sacred trust with their clients! And now thanks to the aberrant behavior of a tiny number of dishonest, *dysfunctional* brokers, the very livelihood of these fine, upstanding, *non-dysfunctional* husbands, daughters, and dads is threatened!" It wasn't exactly what I would have ended up with, but everybody thought it sounded pretty good, and Ted congratulated me for introducing the concept of dysfunction into the mix. And later when Julia presented it to PH&J, they loved it! "Big time!" as Julia said. It was decided that on the day the indictments were announced, PH&J would hold a press conference featuring innocent *non-dysfunctional* brokers with their families. Ted asked me to help Julia with the families, and she was so excited by PH&J's enthusiasm for the idea, she didn't seem to mind. Oh, and I almost forgot. Andrea called after I sent her the fax from the last week or so. She loved the stuff about my family and thinks the job is doing the trick so far as keeping me from obsessing about the book. But then she said something about how I was a sweet, vulnerable person, and she was a little worried about my work environment. I asked her what she meant, and there was another one of those long pauses. After which she said the strangest thing. She said she bets Joanne breaks up with Bob.

TODAY I WILL FILE FOR AN EXTENSION ON MY INCOME TAXES!

I just clean forgot! But that's okay! I am entitled to file for an extension! It's my legal right!

I WILL TRUST MY GUT INSTINCTS!

On the 19th the DA's office will announce their fraud indictments against the four PH&J brokers who took part in the scheme. "Dysfunctional rotten apples," as Julia calls them. Yesterday Julia and I met the three brokers PH&J selected to represent their barrel of non-dysfunctional good apples at our press conference. A husband, a daughter, and a dad. The dad is Ken Knoblauch, whose son, Brent, has muscular dystrophy and was recently confined to a wheelchair, and the Knoblauchs need to build a one-story house for poor Brent. I'm supposed to help Julia prepare the families for the press conference. Basically, they're not supposed to say anything, but if someone asks them a question, they're supposed to say how upset their good apple was at what happened and that they hope people don't stop using PH&J just because of what a few bad apples did. My gut instinct told me that using Brent this way was a big mistake. And I started to say something to Julia and Roger, the guy from PH&J, but Julia told me to shut up. Roger thought the one-story house was a great angle, and Julia agreed. But I think she was uncomfortable, too, because she assigned me to the Knoblauchs. And speaking of gut instincts, Andrea was right! Joanne did leave her boyfriend!

I WILL LISTEN TO MUSIC!

don't think Ken Knoblauch really wants to be at that press conference. It turns out that Patti, Ken's wife, was the one who pushed for it. She told me she hoped it might heighten people's awareness of MD, and that these kind of experiences really help Brent. She showed me around their small two-story house and explained that the doctors said Brent would never walk again, and they really needed to build a one-story house, but that money was really a problem. Then she told me that Brent's disease had really gotten her out of her shell, and that in a way it was the best thing that ever happened to her. I trusted my gut instinct and said I didn't believe that, and she started to cry, so I hugged her. She told me she hadn't had a day off since Brent was diagnosed four years ago. She had wanted to take a weekend with Ken about a month ago and leave Brent at her mother's house, but her mother wouldn't take him because she said Brent's wheelchair leaves marks in her new carpet. And Ken just seems dazed. How Patti keeps going, I don't know. Well, I do know. Because I met Brent. I think he sensed I was feeling sad even though I was pretending not to be, because he asked me if I wanted to listen to music. He put on a tape of "Ramblin' Man" by the Allman Brothers, and in about ten seconds we were singing and dancing around, Brent using his joy stick to go back and forth and whirl around in his wheelchair. After the song was over, I asked him the make, and you know what? It was by the same company I had represented a couple years back! They make a good wheelchair!

TRACE IT, FACE IT, AND ERASE IT! II

I asked the Knoblauchs if I could take Brent for an evening. I don't think Patti and Ken had had a night out for years. But really it was an excuse for me to hang out with Brent, who I like a lot. I told him we could do anything he wanted, because PH&J was paying for it. He made a joke; he said why don't we go out and buy a one-story house. But I don't think it was really a joke. I remember when I was Brent's age, my parents were always arguing about money. For some reason I thought I was somehow responsible. I can only imagine how Brent feels. Brent decided on a place called Medieval Times, this castle where you eat a medieval dinner with your hands and watch knights riding horses and jousting and doing various other chivalrous acts of derring-do. It was great! We sat in the red-and-black section, so we yelled and screamed and cheered for the red-and-black knight, Sir Galahad. It reminded me of something that happened when I was ten. Remember the Ajax White Knight? Well, I was watching *Bonanza* one night, and during the commercial they announced the "Name the White Knight Contest." The winner would get a car *and* a carful of money! That should help things around here! And then the name hit me. Sir Cleanalot! So without telling anybody I rode my bike down to the supermarket the next morning and found the "Name the White Knight Contest" display and entered "Sir Cleanalot!" I was sure I was going to win, and we'd have a new car and a carful of money! All because I picked the absolute perfect name for the Ajax White Knight! Now all I had to do was wait six weeks until they announced the winner on *Bonanza*. The next six weeks went by so slowly. About three weeks in I started to have my doubts. Maybe someone else thought of Sir Cleanalot. Maybe a lot of people did. I mean, it's so obviously the perfect name. But then I checked the rules form, and it said that in the case of a tie, the earliest postmark would win, and since I got mine in at nine in the morning the day after the contest was announced on *Bonanza*, I figured I was okay. I didn't say anything to anybody the whole six weeks until the day of the show. On the bus back from school I told Donnie we had to get the whole family to watch *Bonanza* tonight. He asked me why, so I made him promise not to tell anyone and then told him. He just laughed at me and then told Mom and Dad. Well, you can imagine. Mom said what I had done was sweet and that she hoped I wouldn't be too disappointed when I lost. Dad just ridiculed me. But Jodie thought I had a real shot at winning. I just got angry and more convinced that I was going to win. And I decided that Mom and Dad could have the car, but I was going to keep the money and split it with Jodie. By the time *Bonanza* came on, Dad had started to call me Sir Eatalot, which Donnie thought was hilarious. We sat in the living room, waiting for the last commercial, when the announcement was going to be made. At about 8:55 my heart was pounding and I was trying to block my family out of my consciousness and pray that the name was Sir Cleanalot. Then for the first time the most horrible possibility hit me. What if someone had thought of a *better* name than Sir Cleanalot? What if the very perfectness of Sir Cleanalot made it less exciting as a winning name? What if there was a name almost as perfect, but harder to think of? At 8:57 the commercial came on. The spokesman for Ajax said that over four hundred thousand entries has been made and that the winner was . . . Mrs. Charles Hesby of Council Bluffs, Iowa, and the name she had submitted and the new name of the Ajax White Knight . . . Sir Lancelot. Anyway, our Sir Galahad won the tournament last night. And he beat Sir Lancelot by slitting his throat with some kind of long ax. And Brent really cheered. But not louder than me!

I WILL NOT DRIVE MYSELF CRAZY BY COMPARING MYSELF TO OTHERS. II

Patti told me that on her one night out, she and Ken just argued. Mainly about the press conference, which he just didn't want to do. I gave Patti a copy of Ann Wilson Schaef's *Meditations for Women Who Do Too Much*, because, well, she's a woman and she does too much. She, of course, doesn't think so. As the mother of a sick child I think she thinks it's impossible to do too much. And maybe she's right. Maybe if she stopped, she'd have to face her fears about Brent. When I got the book for Patti, I promised myself not to compare my book with Ann Wilson Schaef's book, and I kept my promise, although hers is much better. But I found that I was comparing myself to Patti, beating myself up for not doing enough. What a set-up! "Hey, Critical Inner Voice, how do I compare with the mother of a crippled child, you know, in terms of selflessness? And while you're at it, who's a better person, me or Mother Teresa!" When I was growing up, my Mom had her antennae out, you know, to catch us in case any of us were, God forbid, having fun. And if we were, she'd stop that, usually by shaming us about how there were starving children in Asia and Africa. Her basic message was that it was better to feel guilty than happy and that as long as we had food on the table it was our duty to overeat it compulsively. Well, I am trying my best through this book to help people who are victims of some very serious diseases. And I refuse to feel guilty or ashamed! Although I probably should do more.

I DESERVE RECOGNITION!

Well, the press conference was a roaring success! The chairman of PH&J announced that the company was cooperating with the DA's office and had suspended the dysfunctional bad apples, and then he introduced the non-dysfunctional good apples. And guess who was the hit?! Brent! He talked about how hard his Dad works, and how much easier a one-story house would make it for his Mom. Then he said he heard somewhere that his Dad's company had offered to pay for the house, and he glanced over and winked at me, because I had told him to say it, which was probably the wrong thing to do. But everyone applauded, especially the chairman, who patted Brent on the head and said that was just what the company was going to do! Afterward we all went out for Cokes and Patti and Brent and Ken were sky-high! So was Julia. And she said the first nice thing she ever said to me. She said that I had been a big help! And you know what I started to say? I started to say, "I don't deserve credit! I didn't know what I was doing! My gut instinct had been that using Brent was a bad idea!" And you know what? I stopped myself. And do you want to know why? Because I was wrong. I did deserve recognition! And then Julia said something that made me feel very good! She said she would be sure to tell Ted!

I WILL NOT GET ENMESHED IN OTHER PEOPLE'S LIVES!

Ted said he heard the press conference had gone well. He didn't say that Julia had told him how big a help I was. He didn't have to! I could tell from the way he asked me to send Joanne flowers. Joanne hasn't talked to me in a while, but I think she and Ted are *seeing* each other, if you know what I mean. In fact, I'm pretty sure of it, because the card on the flowers said, "Let's have sex again real soon!" although it could have been a joke. Or it could have been both. Ted's pretty funny. But I don't have to even think about it. It has nothing to do with me! Too often, those of us who have lived with alcoholics or rage-aholics or whatever, get enmeshed in the lives of the people around us, and forget to put the focus where it belongs! On me! Or us! Whatever!

JOANNE BROKE UP WITH TED.

Joanne is in my bed asleep. It's about seven in the morning and I'm talking down my daily entry. I'll make her coffee before I go. She showed up about midnight last night, crying. She and Ted had this humongous fight because she found out he had been sleeping with his wife! I told her that was impossible, because his wife was suing him for divorce and refusing to let him see the kids. But she told me that she confronted the wife and that the wife broke down and told her that Ted was a womanizer and that he had slept with several hundred women during their marriage, including Julia, Marilee, and Sandy (the receptionist who hates me because she thinks I got her job), and that the reason his wife didn't want him to see the kids was that the kids had known about it and a couple times even covered for him. Talk about your dysfunctional families! So I said, Then why is this woman sleeping with him, and Joanne just said I was naive. And then she started crying again, and I hugged her and brushed her hair. And then Joanne said she was afraid I might lose my job because of this. And I said, "Hey, I am staying out of all this! I refuse to become enmeshed in other people's lives!" It's that simple!

I'VE BEEN FIRED! THE ONLY REASON I GOT THE JOB IN THE FIRST PLACE IS THAT TED'S A SEX ADDICT AND WANTED TO GET INTO JOANNE'S PANTS, AND AS SOON AS SHE WAS OUT OF THE PICTURE I BECAME EXPENDABLE. I CAN'T BELIEVE WHAT AN IDIOT I'VE BEEN! WHY DO I KEEP FOOLING MYSELF, PICKING SICK PEOPLE! I'LL NEVER GET BETTER! I'M JUST HOPELESS! AND I'M TWENTY POUNDS OVERWEIGHT!

I AM NOT TOTALLY WORTHLESS!

The past two weeks have been sheer hell. Talk about your codependent shame spirals! I went to bed, turned off the phone, and holed up with a crate of Oreos. Carl, my OA sponsor, came knocking at my door. So did Andrea, who flew in from New York. She pounded on the door and shouted, "Stuart, I know you're in there! C'mon, Stuart! You can *choose* to feel good!" Boy, did that sound hollow! I told her to go away, but she refused. She shouted, "Stuart, you are good enough!" I said go away! She said, "Stuart, would you get off your own back!" When I didn't answer, she just shouted, "Stuart, don't you think you're being a bit ridiculous?!" And I shouted, "Yes, I'm a ridiculous person. Now go away!" And she did. But she came back with Carl. Now they were both out there shouting slogans at me. "Progress, not perfection," the Three C's (I didn't cause it, I can't control it, and I can't cure it), the Three A's (Awareness, Acceptance, Action). I wouldn't budge. And finally they went away. But they came back. With Brent. And his parents, Patti and Ken. Which was a dirty trick. So I let everybody in and gave them Oreos. The Knoblauchs told me they came to say thank you. And good-bye. PH&J is building their one-story house in Orlando, where the firm has some offices, because Brent wants to live near Disney World. Then Ken took me aside and told me the weirdest thing. He said he had been one of the bad apples. That a few times he had shorted one of his clients. An orthodontist. It was only a couple thousand dollars, but he had been desperate. He told the orthodontist and is paying him back and the orthodontist still wants him to be his broker. I thought back to when I first judged the brokers who had stolen from their clients and called them low-life scum. And how I wondered what weirdness might have caused them to do something like that. Who knows why people do dishonest things or destructive things or even cruel things? But I knew Ken Knoblauch would never do something like that again. So I showed Brent how to twist open an Oreo so there's creme left on both halves, made him promise to come visit me, and got dressed.

FAIL TO PLAN, PLAN TO FAIL!

Actually, the biggest shock when I opened that door was seeing Andrea. She must have lost about eighty or ninety pounds. And when I offered everybody Oreos, she refused. She was smart. She knew I'd have junk food, and brought her own lunch (pasta salad and melon balls). As we say in OA, "Fail to Plan, Plan to Fail!" And is it ever true! How many times have I fallen off the wagon because I didn't plan ahead. . . . Gee, I forgot to prepare a healthy, measured lunch. I wonder what's quick and easy? Maybe pizza. You know, with broccoli on top. Just a slice. Actually, as I say it, that sounds pretty good. But sorry, Mr. Pizza Man, I know what I'm having for lunch today. Pasta salad and melon balls!

I AM AN ATTRACTIVE PERSON!

Which I am not. Wait a minute. I'm sorry. That's exactly wrong. And exactly the opposite of what I'm saying here. And it's Stinkin' Thinkin'! Yes, I put on some significant Oreo weight, and I am pushing two hundred pounds! And when I pass by a store window and look at myself, I see a fat slob. But that's okay! No, it isn't. Because it will make me even more nuts, which will make me want to deaden the pain with food. So next time I look at me in that store window, I am going to say, "Hey, that guy is . . . well, not Mel Gibson, but a reasonably attractive guy!" Besides, attractiveness is a very subjective thing. And if you project attractiveness, you will be attractive! Just look at the Elephant Man! He was hideous-looking, but a very sensitive and wonderful person, and people—some people who really got to know him—found him to be an attractive person to be around. And I understand that his left hand was really beautiful. A friend of mine is a photographer for catalogs, and he shoots a lot of watches and rings and uses a lot of hand models, people who have beautiful hands. He told me that the Elephant Man's left hand was legendarily beautiful and that if he were alive today, the Elephant Man could be a hand model! So think about it: If the Elephant Man could be a model, how hard is it to say, "I am an attractive person!"

FIRST THINGS FIRST! IV

When we say first things first in the program we mean that we can't do everything at once. We need to take just one step at a time and start with what is really important. Yesterday I decided to sit down and meditate and find out what my Higher Power thought was most important for me to do. Should I look for another job? Should I maybe take a writing course so that I know what I'm doing? Is it time for me to, God forbid, try to get involved in a relationship? So I sat down on my living room rug and closed my eyes. As usual, I was having problems blanking out the world, so I got up and put on a tape of ocean waves crashing onto the beach, and sat down again. Well, of course I started thinking about this terrible vacation I had with Dale, my rage-aholic ex, so I got up and put on a tape of crickets, sat down, and well, would you like a multiple choice? A. The camping trip where Dad got drunk and lost Jodie. B. The camping trip where Dad got drunk and lost Donnie. C. The camping trip where Dad got drunk and lost me. D. All of the above. So I got up and put on a tape of this meditation flute music, and sat down, and then the phone rang. It was a wrong number, so I sat down again, and you know what? I was huffing and puffing. And I thought, this is it! I gotta get back in shape! *Today I will exercise!*

TODAY I WILL STRETCH!

Okay. I am not twenty years old anymore. Although, now that I said it, when I was twenty I weighed nearly three hundred pounds and running a mile like I did yesterday would have killed me, or whomever I landed on when I collapsed. Anyway, I am a forty-year-old formerly obese white American male with questionable body tone and flexibility. And I am in such pain I cannot tell you. So if you get nothing more out of this book, remember, first things first! Stre-e-e-e-e-tch!!!

TODAY I WILL CONSULT
A PHYSICIAN!

I was about ten when my Dad started getting on me for "taking up too much space." So they put me on this diet. And that's when I started sneaking food, at night, at friends' houses, at school, at the Dairy Queen. And I just gained weight. Well, that convinced Mom that something was wrong with my thyroid or my metabolism or something and she decided she wanted to take me to a doctor, which Dad was against because it cost money and he was convinced I was just sneaking food like he would sneak booze when he was supposed to be on the wagon. So after a lot of arguing, Mom finally took me to the doctor, who, of course, said there was nothing wrong with me, which led to even more screaming and hollering at home about money and my eating and Dad's drinking and the whole nine yards. As you can imagine, this did wonders for my sense of entitlement to the various professional health care services! And it's true that many of us with addictive attitudes don't believe we are worth being taken care of. Most of us wouldn't treat our car as badly as we treat ourselves. If something's wrong with the transmission, we take it in. But if something's wrong with our body, well, it can wait. Now, at one point in my life, I would have read that and said, "You know, he's right. I probably shouldn't take my car in so frequently. I deserve to break down at rush hour and have thousands of people scream at me for holding up traffic!" But I realize now that my body is my most important possession, because it's the only one made by God, unless I had a pet, which I don't. Although I would like one, probably a cat, because I live in an apartment. Anyway, my body is a temple or a church or a synagogue or whatever, a Christian Science Reading Room, I don't know. Which makes me think . . . okay . . .

* IF I AM FORTY OR OVER, I WILL CONSULT MY HIGHER POWER BEFORE STARTING A STRENUOUS NEW EXERCISE REGIMEN, BECAUSE I COULD GET HEART PALPITATIONS AND EXTREME SHORTNESS OF BREATH.

---

* alternate May 12 affirmation for Christian Scientists

I DON'T HAVE TO LIVE FROM CRISIS TO CRISIS! III

Okay. The doctor put me on a walk a mile, jog a half mile, walk a mile program and I'm feeling fine. I don't have to be Jane Fonda. Thank God! Not that she isn't a wonderful, talented person. I mean, did you see *Klute*?! But you know what? I'm glad I'm Stuart! The other day, Carl, my OA sponsor, said something that made me feel so good. I was moaning about something or other—what a bad hand I was dealt in life—and he said, "Stuart, can you think of one person you would trade places with?" And guess what. I couldn't think of anyone. Sure I'd like to dance like Baryshnikov or sing like Barry Manilow, but when it comes right down to it, I'd rather be Stuart with all my problems and all my grief than be Mikhail or Barry with all their problems and all their grief, although I hope they have none, they have given so much of themselves for so long. Anyway, I am exercising; I am eating healthy; I am writing this book; I am thinking about maybe writing my résumé or taking a course; and I am glad I'm me! And for right now, that's enough! I don't need a crisis in my life to make it worth living.

MY BROTHER IS SUING MY SISTER!

Okay. I wish all you readers could just go to coffee with me and I could explain this whole thing. This is just one of those real-life situations that's too complicated for a single daily affirmation entry (although that hasn't stopped me so far!). But I'll do my best, that's all I can do, and that's good enough, and it's okay. Okay. *First of all, I am going home!* I know. But they need me. My sister, Jodie, called yesterday in tears. The family is going nuts over, surprise, *money*. The Smalleys have never been very good with money. Dad grew up during the Depression. His mother's! Actually, that's a joke I heard from a very funny comedian, Vince Gerardi, who is part of a group called Comedians in Recovery, so Vince, I owe you an amends, unless you don't mind, in which case . . . Anyway, the money in question is Aunt Paula's and now that she's gone, everybody thinks it's theirs. Or at least a chunk of it. Of course, we're talking about maybe a grand total of fifty-odd thousand dollars here, most of which is tied up in Aunt Paula's house, which is a big part of the problem. Aunt Paula had, fortunately, made out a will and designated Jodie as the executor of her estate because Jodie took care of Aunt Paula when she was sick and Aunt Paula really loved her. Mom thinks Jodie is incapable of being the executor because basically she thinks Jodie is incapable of anything. Donnie thinks he should be the executor because he's the oldest kid and he used to fix Aunt Paula's car, a fact I believe he intends to use in court. Dad, of course, felt he should be the executor, even though, as Donnie pointed out, for the last twenty years Aunt Paula would leave any room he walked into. Anyway, Jodie felt capable of handling Aunt Paula's estate because of all the experience she's had dealing with her divorce. (She just got a restraining order preventing her husband from coming within a hundred yards of her Accord.) So, quite uncharacteristically, Jodie held her ground over the objections of everyone, except me (I was incommunicado eating Oreos), and exercised her prerogative to be executor. Now it turns out that Donnie saw his ten thousand dollars plus change as a chance to get out of Mom and Dad's house and make a down payment on a cheap house, a cheap two-bedroom house like Aunt Paula's. And, of course, Jodie saw it as her opportunity to move herself and Kyle, her boy, out of their cruddy little apartment and into . . . a cheap two-bedroom house. Okay, I'm going to save the rest till tomorrow because it involves Minnesota probate law and something about an easement. And I feel like I'm getting into "facts not feelings," and basically, everybody in my family is feeling angry and betrayed and hurt and resentful and just plain pissed off. And I'm flying there in an hour!

WHEN I FLY HOME TO VISIT MY FAMILY I WILL RENT A CAR!!!!!!!!!!

Which I will do later today. I have to get out of here! I've been in this house less than a day, and I'm already crazy! I could go sleep on Jodie's couch, but that would be deemed as taking her side. If I stayed in a motel, Dad and Mom would be pissed off, and if I'm going to referee this thing, I need everybody's cooperation. Why is everything in this family about taking sides? Mom is on Jodie's side, so even though Donnie lives here and we're sleeping in the same room, this is considered neutral territory, especially considering that Donnie suspects I like Jodie better, which is true. Dad is on Donnie's side, and he and Mom are either not talking or on each other. Last night we had a lightning storm, and they reenacted this horrific scene from my childhood. For some God-knows-what reason, Mom is terrified of lightning. She thinks it's going to come into the house and electrocute us. So she ran around the house unplugging all the appliances. Dad was drunk and followed her, plugging everything back in and laughing at her. This used to happen when I was a kid, and I guess for some reason I'd blocked it. But take a wild guess. How do you think I feel during a thunderstorm? Answer. Not happy! I just gotta get out of here!

I DON'T HAVE TO KEEP SCORE!

By now I've heard more or less everybody's version of this whole dispute and I am totally disgusted with each and every member of my family. First of all, this is infinitely more complicated than what I told you the other day. But in a way the whole thing is very simple—and it boils down to this—*everybody in my family keeps score*. In their heads. I know how it works, because I'm guilty of it too. "I'll do such-and-such for you, but in return I expect such-and-such somewhere down the line." And the most important part of keeping score, the *only* important part, is that the score has to be exactly even. But it never is! Because the score is kept silently on your Inner Scoreboard. That way everybody's scoreboard has a different total from everybody else's, and in their own minds, everybody feels they're getting the short end and resents the hell out of it! . . . I really don't know where to begin. Maybe with Aunt Paula's furniture, or the coin collection, or Donnie's lawyer. Maybe I should just start with Dad. Dad is not the world's most trusting person. He took me aside yesterday in the garage and told me that Jodie has already stolen a good deal of our vast inheritance by soaking Aunt Paula before she died. Evidently, while Jodie was taking care of her, Aunt Paula lent Jodie money because Jodie was having the trouble with her husband and has Kyle to raise. And, of course, Jodie never paid her back, which is totally understandable. Now Jodie told me last night in her car that we're talking maybe five or six thousand dollars here, but Dad has it blown up to thirty and Donnie has it at about forty. Jodie, of course, feels she earned every penny of it. And as long as we're talking about feelings, Donnie's lawyer feels Jodie has to account for every cent Aunt Paula gave her. If, as Jodie claims, some of those checks were "reimbursements" for groceries, well, Jodie should have receipts! Donnie's lawyer is a Navy buddy of Donnie's, which in Donnie's case means an old drinking and smoking buddy, and he's not charging Donnie anything, which I guess is a nice thing to do. Jodie's lawyer, who charges seventy-five dollars an hour on her divorce and fifty dollars an hour on this thing because he's not a probate expert, feels that the grocery receipt issue is just a harassment tactic, part of a pattern to inflate Jodie's legal bills. But Jodie says she'd rather her lawyer get the money than Donnie and is willing to spend every cent fighting him. See. As long as the score is even. Better zero to zero than a thousand to nine hundred and ninety-nine. As for me? Well, everybody's buttering me up. Mom says she wants to read the book, and she's sure it's great and will sell a million copies! Gee, thanks, Mom, for *really* believing in me. (That was sarcastic—I must be angry!) And Jodie! She picked me up yesterday to discuss this whole thing, and *she takes me to an OA meeting.* I've been trying to get her to a meeting for years, and this is her way of getting me on her side. I don't think she heard a word anyone said, but at the end she said OA was the greatest thing since whole-wheat pasta and it was going to change her life. I could just see the numbers spinning on Jodie's Inner Scoreboard. And Mom's. And Dad's and Donnie's.

I WILL STAY AWAY FROM PEOPLE, PLACES, AND THINGS THAT MAKE ME CRAZY!

Donnie took me out for a burger last night to explain his side of the dispute over Aunt Paula's house. He says living with Mom and Dad is driving him nuts, and that's why he's smoking pot and drinking. But right now he's living off his Navy pension and can't really afford to move out. Donnie's tried to quit drinking and drugging a number of times. I think he's been in about four or five Navy hospitals for rehab. But sooner or later, something would happen and he'd fall off the wagon. I remember once he was released from rehab and they reassigned him to this minuscule island in the Pacific, where there were about thirty-two indigenous people and ten Navy guys. Well, they made Donnie head of supply, and one of his duties was, of course, dispensing the liquor! In AA they have a saying, "People, places, and things," meaning stay away from people, places, and things that might threaten your sobriety. From the stories I've heard, I would put on that list Navy People, Army Places, and Marine Things! Well, in OA, Al-Anon, DA, and ACOA we have the same slogan. And I'm sitting here in the worst possible place, the home I grew up in; with the worst possible people, the Smalleys; and staring at the worst possible things, everything in this place that reminds me of these people! I mean, this morning I yelled at Mom for some stupid reason, and I didn't even make an immediate amends. I must have waited two hours. Carl, my OA sponsor, thinks I'm crazy to be here. And so does Andrea. But you know what? The slogan helps. Because at least I realize that I'm feeling this way because I'm here in this house, and I know that I don't have to stay here forever. Although it might seem like it!

TODAY I REFUSE TO BE OVERWHELMED!!

Okay. Let me see if I can explain this in a nutshell. Jodie, as executor, decided that *she* would buy Aunt Paula's house and that each of us, Mom, Dad, Donnie, Jodie, and me, would receive one fifth of the purchase price, with Jodie using her share as her down payment. Which is fine, except that Donnie also wanted the house, so he's mad. Then there's the easement. Evidently, when the house was originally surveyed, someone did a bad job, and two feet of Aunt Paula's driveway is on her neighbor's property. So we need an easement from Aunt Paula's neighbor before the bank will give Jodie a mortgage. The neighbor, Mr. Egeberg, wanted three thousand for the easement, which Donnie claims Jodie agreed to without consulting the rest of the family. But Jodie's lawyer told me he informed Donnie's lawyer in writing several times before Jodie finally agreed to the three thousand and gave me a copy of his file, which shows the whole history of the correspondence between him and Donnie's lawyer, and I'm having a little trouble working my way through it without getting overwhelmed. Anyway, after Jodie insisted that the three thousand dollars for the easement come out of everyone's share of the inheritance, Donnie pulled up with a U-Haul and emptied out Aunt Paula's house—just stripped it, and he's storing stuff in Mom and Dad's garage and basement. So right now I'm sitting in the basement, staring at Aunt Paula's home entertainment center, which must be twenty years old. It feels kind of weird down here. Dad used to "putter" in the basement before he started "puttering" in the garage. Every once in a while he actually would putter—making some odd thing. When I was about sixteen, he got on this kick of filling wine bottles with colored stones and making lamps out of them. Talk about denial! Mom got all excited about the lamps and put them all over the house, which was just what we needed—more constant reminders that Dad was a drunk! *You* try concentrating on your homework when your dad is raging around the house and you're reading from the light of a Gallo wine bottle. To this day I think the Karamazov Brothers are Ernest and Julio!! And I'll tell you, I still feel overwhelmed when I sit down to read something I'm not sure I understand. Which is why maybe I can't concentrate on this file of documents in front of me and why maybe I should at least use a different lamp.

TODAY IT'S OKAY TO FEEL LOSS.

I can't seem to stay away from this basement. I keep seeing memories, and the weird thing is, they're not all bad memories. I think in their whole lives Mom and Dad have thrown away just one thing, Donnie's baseball card collection. Actually, Mom didn't throw them away; she shredded them and used them as a mulch for her tomatoes. Donnie was so mad! Those cards meant so much to him. And me. Donnie and I would ride our bikes up to the Texa-Tonka superette and spend all our money on baseball cards. Then we'd sit on the curb and Donnie would blow these huge bubbles, which I've never been able to do. And I thought he was the coolest big brother in the world. Donnie would let me organize his cards, which we kept in this shoe box, and I'd advise Donnie on all his trades. I remember once we had triples on Reno Bertoia, a third baseman who hit maybe .230 for the Twins, and Craig Strobel came over with his cards. Craig, whose family, by the way, was extremely dysfunctional (but that's another story), Craig only cared about the Twins. So I got Donnie a Whitey Ford for one of the extra Reno Bertoias and a Warren Spahn for the other! When Craig left, Donnie and I were just rolling around laughing. Now I can't talk to him without my skin crawling. But I have to remember it's not Donnie who's making my skin crawl. It's his disease. The other Donnie is in there somewhere. And I miss him. But that's okay! Maybe while I'm here, I'll take in a Twins game. I really should rent that car.

TODAY I WILL REMEMBER THAT IT'S A CUNNING, BAFFLING, POWERFUL DISEASE!

It occurred to me that Jodie's seven-year-old son, Kyle, doesn't have any positive male role models, so yesterday I decided to finally rent that car and take him to a Twins game. Jodie's husbands have all seemed to have come out of the same cookie cutter. They were all kind of shy, but in an upbeat, friendly way at first, and then by the end, these raging monsters came out. Jimmy, Jodie's third and current husband, was really terrific at first, especially with Kyle, whose real dad, Jodie's second husband, Ace, moved his landscaping business to Wisconsin when Kyle was two. But now Jimmy's on this rampage, spying on Jodie and doing everything he can to sabotage her life. He's been pretty cunning about it and hasn't slashed her tires since she got the restraining order to keep him at least a hundred yards from her Accord. Anyway, I thought it might do Kyle some good to hear the crack of the bat, have a couple hot dogs, maybe some peanuts and Cracker Jack, an ice-cold Coke, some nachos, and one of those chocolate malted ice-cream cups—you know, really experience a major league baseball game! So I rented a Capri from Budget, picked Kyle up, and took him downtown to the Metrodome. I never really liked playing baseball—I was always the last one picked—but I've always loved watching it. Especially keeping score. So I got us both programs and taught Kyle how to score the game, and I'll tell you, the kid is incredibly smart! We even had a 6-4-3-2 double play, which he figured out himself! I guess keeping score must run in the Smalley genes! The Twins beat the Indians 12–2 in a laugher, but we waited till the very last out before heading down to the parking lot, where we found my rented Capri, the tires slashed.

IT'S NOT ALL BLACK AND WHITE!

Staying here at home, I am beginning to feel that I have two choices. Either I can decide to move back here and try to solve everybody's problems (as if I could!), or I can decide never to come back and just forget these people (as if I could!). Everything I've learned in program tells me to leave. Every time I think of Kyle seeing those slashed tires, I think I should stay. But you know what? This is my disease talking! Those of us with addictive attitudes tend to see things in black and white. Either/or. And whichever way I decide is wrong. If I stay, it means I'm a grandiose fool, setting myself up for failure and certain insanity. If I leave, I'm a heartless, selfish ingrate. So there are my choices . . . Grandiose Fool or Heartless Creep. Talk about Stinkin' Thinkin'!! Well, doggone it! I don't have to choose! I can be *both*!

I CAN CHANGE, I CAN COPE, AND I CAN CELEBRATE!!! (THE NEW THREE C'S)

Yesterday was Kyle's eighth birthday, and Jodie threw a party for him. Mainly it was kids from his school and his swimming club. (The kid's a fish!) But Mom and I came, as did a few of Jodie's friends from work. (As a precaution she had us all park within a hundred yards of her Accord.) The party was great! The kids are at that terrific age where one minute they can act so grown-up and the next minute be so infantile. Sounds like they're forty! It really was a celebration! And I needed it! (Though I didn't need those three pieces of Jodie's birthday cake—it was so good!) It's just that I've been under so much stress here, I look around at my family and keep reciting the three *C*'s: I didn't *Cause* it; I can't *Control* it; and I can't *Cure* it! And then I realize how negative that sounds. Well, here are three *positive C*'s. I can *Change!* I can *Cope!* And yes, I can *Celebrate!* . . . Also, I can *Cook* low-*Calorie* foods, because I really ate too much *Cake*.

THERE IS MORE THAN ONE RIGHT WAY!!

Growing up in my house, there was Dad's Way and the Wrong Way. Unless Mom was mad at Dad. Then there was Dad's Way and the Right Way, which was Mom's Way. That's, of course, if Dad wasn't right there in the room. If Dad was close by, there was Dad's Way and the Dangerous Way. If I just got you a little confused, that's okay! I was confused too. Many of us with codependent attitudes are absolutely desperate to do things the right way. But it seems the more desperate we are, the harder it is to figure out what the right way is. And sometimes it helps to remember that there is no right way, or better yet there are many different right ways. For example, right now I'm working on a little project. Aunt Paula collected literally thousands of coins, mainly pennies, you know, wheat pennies and some Indian heads, but also hundreds of dimes and quite a few Liberty silver dollars. And she kept these things in, you know, Sucrets boxes and Ziploc bags, it was just a big, humongous mess. Well, when Donnie emptied out Aunt Paula's with the U-Haul, he got these coins and brought them all to a coin expert, who said they were worth a couple hundred dollars. But Mom said Donnie was stupid because he brought them all in a big paper bag, and that started a big fight. Anyway, I volunteered to take a little time and organize these things, which perhaps may enhance their value, and perhaps not. I don't know. I know nothing about coins. So I'm sitting here in the kitchen and I'm sorting these thousands of pennies and putting them individually into these teeny little clear plastic—I don't know, Baggies, coin Baggies, clear envelopes—I don't know what you call them. And I'm wondering is this the right way to do this, and Dad walks in and makes fun of me. And I just have to remember, I'm doing this the right way!

TODAY I WILL FEEL MY OWN FEELINGS!

I finished my project and went downtown and got the coins appraised by a numismatist, a coin expert. He said that they were worth about two hundred and fifty dollars. He told me that sorting them wasn't really a waste of time, because it saved him the trouble of doing it himself. Driving home, I started to worry about how everyone would react to this news. Would Mom be mad that I showed that Donnie hadn't done a bad job in the first place? Would Donnie be appreciative or just get angry at Mom again? And would there be an argument or would he just drive off on his motorcycle? Maybe it'd be no big deal, or maybe everyone will thank me for the effort I went to, and Mom'll make me a turkey sandwich while I sit in the living room and watch a movie with Donnie and Dad. That's when I realized that *I was not feeling my own feelings!* Too often those of us with codependent tendencies lose touch with our own feelings and just react to the feelings of those around us. When I first got into recovery, I didn't realize that I even had my own feelings. At the time I was living with Dale, my rage-aholic, and I remember coming home to that apartment, getting off the elevator thinking, "I wonder how I'm going to feel tonight." If Dale was happy, I'd be happy. If Dale was angry, I'd be scared. Then, thanks to program, I realized that I have my own feelings. And not only do I have my own feelings, I have feelings *about* my feelings!! And feelings about my feelings about my feelings!!! And feelings about my feelings about my feelings about my feelings!!!!

TODAY I WILL FEEL MY FEELINGS ABOUT MY FEELINGS ABOUT MY FEELINGS ABOUT MY FEELINGS!!!

Okay. I just read yesterday's entry again, and I have to say that I feel sad. But that's okay. Because I feel sad because I see what's going on with my family and because, frankly, I miss Dale. Which makes me feel angry! I'm angry that I should feel sad about someone who yelled at me constantly. So I'm angry about feeling sad, which is my feeling about my feelings. And you know what? That makes me feel good. Because it shows me how far I've come. So I feel good about being angry about being sad, which is my feelings about my feelings about my feelings. And that makes me sad again, because in spite of how far I've come, I can't seem to figure out how to save my family, which I'm not really supposed to do anyway. Okay. Now I'm getting a little confused. Which is my feelings about my feelings about my feelings about my feelings . . . I think.

TODAY I WILL KEEP IT SIMPLE!

Sometimes we get ourselves all bollixed up. For instance, I'm still trying to read this file from Jodie's lawyer, and the harder I try to figure all this out, the more confused I get. Today I will just let go and read the file without trying to figure it out. I will keep it simple. I will just read it!

I CAN SEE THINGS THROUGH TO THE END!

Andrea thinks I should leave home and go home. I mean, you know what I mean. She called up immediately after reading the last week's pages and said she thinks I'm going crazy here, and that if I don't leave I'm going to end up in bed again. I told her I appreciated her concern and that she was probably right, except that I think I've just made some progress in sorting this whole thing out. Reading through the file, it finally dawned on me that Donnie's lawyer, either by design or through sheer laziness, is not responding to Jodie's lawyer's letters, and that is just bollixing everything up. I told Andrea that for some reason Donnie *wants* to believe Jodie is doing something wrong. Jodie tried calling Donnie a couple times, but they just end up screaming at each other. Andrea said that this was just her point, that I was getting way too enmeshed in my family drama, which I agreed with, except that now that I've gotten this far, I might as well finish it. Because I think I've figured out how to resolve this. Then Andrea said that I didn't have to resolve it in Minnesota, that I could go home and handle it over the phone. Then I said very sarcastically, "Who are you, my editor or my sponsor?" And then I made an immediate amends. But then she said that she *was* my editor and that one of the reasons she wanted me to leave Minnesota was that she felt that the book was suffering, that some of the days' affirmations were getting a little long and dense. At which point I just freaked out! And then Andrea said she just said that because she thought it might get me to leave, and then she made an immediate amends, saying she was sorry she resorted to that kind of manipulation, but that she's really worried about me, even though that's no excuse. I accepted her amends, even though I was still a little freaked out. But then I felt better, because I think I finally got a handle on the situation!

TODAY I CAN LET GO OF THE RESULT!

I once heard that in an Al-Anon meeting. So often we so worry about the result of an action that we end up never taking that action, even when it is something we really need to do. This concept really freed me, because, as I discovered, sometimes just taking the action *is* the result. For example, asking for a raise. If I go into my boss's office all worried about the result, I am going to be tongue-tied and sweaty and nervous that I'm saying exactly the right thing, exactly the right way, and chances are my boss is going to think to himself, "Why should I give a raise to this nervous, tongue-tied sweatbox?" Whereas if I let go of the *result* and realize, "I am entitled to a raise. Therefore I will simply ask for a raise in a very straightforward manner, letting go of the result, and at the very least I will have shown up for myself," And your employer just might think, "Hey, this person is not a sniveling cow with no self-esteem. I like this person! I think I'll give this person a raise!" Or he might not. But that's okay! You at least showed up for yourself, and that is a humongous step on the road to recovery! Well, today I have to remind myself to let go of the result when it comes to my family. That way I can take the actions I feel I need to take. Which are: preparing a detailed chronology of key events which have created and exacerbated this dispute; preparing a clear and concise presentation of the issues still confronting the settlement of Aunt Paula's estate; the Xeroxing and distribution of said preparations; and the calling of a family meeting to quietly and calmly resolve said issues. I'm not going to kid myself. This isn't necessarily going to end with everybody hugging and apologizing and crying and getting into program. But that's okay! I owe it to myself to try.

TODAY I DON'T HAVE TO BE GRANDIOSE!

Carl, my OA sponsor, called. We hadn't talked in a while, and he said he just wanted to know how I was doing. I told him how much I'm getting done. Yesterday I prepared the Chronology and the Definition of Issues. Everyone will be getting their copy tonight to give them a chance to read it before the family meeting tomorrow. Carl then told me he had talked to Andrea, who had kind of filled him in on what was going on, and that he was a little worried that I was trying to control things here. I got a little angry and said I hadn't given him permission to talk to my editor. And he reminded me that he and Andrea had met trying to get me out of bed, which he was grateful for, because the two of them kind of hit it off and were talking a lot over the phone, and that maybe it was a little grandiose of me to think I could grant him permission to talk to another human being, particularly another OA member. At which point I got very defensive and just lashed out, "Oh, I see, so you thirteenth-stepped her!" which is a very ugly program expression for a veteran twelve-step program member sleeping with a newcomer, and I made an amends a nanosecond after it was out of my mouth, but I still felt so ashamed. And Carl said that was all right, and that maybe my being enmeshed in this family crisis was bringing up a lot of shame for me. And that control and grandiosity were just defenses against shame. And then I said yes, yes, yes, you're right!!! God, you're a great sponsor! Why haven't I been calling you?! I'm so ashamed! And then Carl said no, that's okay. And then I said maybe I should call off the family meeting and just leave and let them figure it out. But then I thought maybe it was grandiose to call off a meeting everybody was already planning to go to. Who am I to call off a meeting?! And Carl said that whatever I decided was okay. Just be careful, he said, not to fall into being the hero.

I DON'T HAVE TO BE THE HERO!

When I was four or five we lived in this small apartment building for a while. And one day the superintendent took Donnie's football away from him because he was playing in the wrong place or something. Every kid just hated this superintendent, and we called him Mean Mr. Dimmit. Well, when my Dad got home from work, Donnie told him about it, and Dad charged off to find Mr. Dimmit and get Donnie's football back. On the way, we picked up this trail of kids who wanted to see this, and in front of everyone, Dad told off Mean Mr. Dimmit and got Donnie's football back. I remember that night all of us just glowing with pride as Donnie and Dad and I recounted the victorious confrontation for Mom and Jodie, while Dad held on to that football in his big strong hands. Dad was our hero. At least that night. And I don't know, maybe that's how I got the idea that being a hero is the neatest thing a guy can be. Most of my adult life I've had a recurring dream. Dad is up on the roof. I don't know what he's doing really. Cleaning the gutters, reshingling, I just don't know. But he's been drinking. And in very slow motion he falls back. Off the roof. And, of course, I catch him. And then comes the most vivid part of the dream. I'm holding Dad in my arms. And he looks up at me, and he's really wasted. But he's not angry at all. His eyes just look into mine, and seem to say I'm sorry I'm so helpless, thank you for saving me, I love you. And that's the end. The family meeting is today. It'll be in the kitchen at noon. I decided not to distribute the Chronology or the Definition of Issues. I don't think they were a waste of time. Preparing them helped me organize my thoughts. But I don't want to force myself on everybody, and I want to give everybody a chance to contribute in their own way. You know, give them the dignity of that. Because maybe in the way I've been trying to control this, I haven't been giving them the respect they deserve. And by trying to be the hero, I'm robbing myself of the dignity that I rob Dad of in my dream.

I AM THE NEW EXECUTOR!

Well, the meeting went better than could possibly be hoped. Mom made baked beans and buns, which may become the official traditional Smalley probate lunch. I think everybody was as tense as I was, and the food kind of broke the ice. At first Jodie and Donnie couldn't even look at each other, and I thought that as soon as one said anything to the other, they'd just explode. But after a while, Jodie asked Donnie to pass the diet Coke and then Donnie asked Jodie how Kyle was doing with his swimming, and things loosened up. In fact, this was probably the nicest, most functional interaction we've had in years. Basically, I verbally ran down the summary of the Chronology, which I had, in fact, committed to memory, emphasizing that no one was really at fault other than maybe Donnie's lawyer, who was probably acting out of the best of intentions, and then added that maybe Jodie had overreacted a few times, as had Donnie and Mom and Dad *and* myself, and that we all wanted the same thing, and then I ended with, "There's more at stake here than just dollars and cents. There's a family at stake. A family that loves each other." And then Dad said, "Oh. See, all along I thought you were talking about *our* family." And everybody just fell down laughing. Anyway, it all went great. And we ended up deciding that I should be the new executor. See what can happen when you let go of the result, your grandiosity, and your need to be a hero? It's a miracle!

I WILL NOT BE OVERWHELMED! II

I can get overwhelmed at the drop of a hat. And now that I'm the executor, there's so much to do! I made a list last night in my little black weekly planner-slash-address book, which is a great thing. It's small enough so I can always keep it in my back pocket and I have all my phone numbers and addresses and lists of everything I do. My whole life is in there, right in my back pocket. Anyway, I am looking at the list now, and I have so much to do! Today I'm interviewing new lawyers. I think as executor I should get some advice. I'm going to call Mr. Egeberg, Aunt Paula's neighbor, and try to renegotiate the ease-ment on the driveway. I'm taking the coin collection to a numis-matist in St. Paul to get a third opinion. You know, just to let everyone know that I was thorough. And that's just the tip of the iceberg! If I'm not careful, I will become overwhelmed. And when I become overwhelmed, I find that I lose touch with the moment, because instead of keeping my eye on the task at hand, I get nervous and start thinking about what I have to do next. And then I'm just not present, and then life just becomes pure hell. So thank God I am in recovery and can be aware of this issue. And I have decided to take an action today toward the avoidance of being overwhelmed. And that is that I am going to ask Mom to do my laundry. I have been doing my own laundry here because I didn't want to be any trouble and frankly because I like doing my laundry a certain way. And that's okay. But I am going to ask Mom to do my laundry, and if it's not exactly the way I like it, that's okay. It's a small price to pay for my serenity! So right now I'll just put my little black book with my life in it back in my back pocket and go ask Mom if she'll do my laundry this week.

TODAY I FEEL GOOD ABOUT ME!

I'm so excited about how much I got done yesterday that I got up early and went for a walk-jog-walk this morning. I had kind of gotten out of the habit of exercising here, and I think I'm going to need to be in shape if I'm going to get everything I need to get done, done. So I just showered and I'm sitting here in my room in my underwear and I just wanted to get this affir . . . No, Mom, that's clean. . . . Mom just walked in. . . . Yeah, that's dirty. But keep it separate, it might bleed. . . . I know you know. . . . Mom, I'm not saying . . . Okay, I'm sorry. . . . No, you're right, if I asked you to do it for me, the least I can do is let you do it your way. . . . Fine, do whatever, I'm sorry. . . . Anyway, where was I? Oh, I'm feeling very good about how much I accomplished yesterday. The numismatist in St. Paul thought— It's my daily affirmation, Mom. Daily affirmation, it's my book . . . Mom, I've told you about this a million times. I've been here three weeks, Mom, and I do this every day. It's my book. . . . I'm not yelling. . . . I did *not* wake up on the wrong side of the bed today! . . . Okay. I'm sorry. I apologize. I'm sorry. . . . No. that's clean, Mom. I just wore those last night for my Al-Anon meeting. Look, maybe I should just do my own . . . No, you're right. Just do it your way. That's fine. It's better. It's better than my way . . . No, I'm not being sarcastic . . . I'm sorry if it sounded sarcastic. I truly meant that your way is probably as good if not better than my way. I just didn't want you to wash pants that were still basically clean . . . No, you're right. Just take the belt out of th— I'm sorry, I know you're not going to wash a belt. I know that. I'm sorry. I must have been temporarily insane. . . . No, I am not being sarcastic. I really appreciate your doing my laundry. Thank you, Mom. Really, thanks. You're making everything a lot easier for me. . . . No, I'm not being sarcastic. . . .

GOD GRANT ME THE SERENITY TO ACCEPT THE THINGS I CANNOT CHANGE!

My weekly planner-slash-address book is gone. Shredded and dissolved in Mom's washing machine. Nothing will bring it back. All my phone numbers are gone. I cannot change that. They're gone. All the notes, all the records of my meetings, all my lists, they're gone. They're just gone. I cannot go back in time and take the book out of my back pocket before Mom put it in the washer. And screaming at Mom would not bring my little book back. My little black book is gone. I will never see it again. That I cannot change.

I WILL REACH OUT TO OTHERS.

I went to an Al-Anon meeting last night and shared. And as usual, everyone was very helpful. During the break, a few people came up to me and helped me realize that I had still not accepted the loss of my weekly planner-slash-address book. And that that was the reason I have been unable to take the actions I need to take as executor of Aunt Paula's estate. At coffee afterwards, Stan, a really great guy whose wife has been sober two years, suggested I go out and buy a new book tomorrow. And I realized that I had been afraid to buy a new book. That I thought that just because my old book had been swallowed up and destroyed, that that would happen to my next book too. Talk about Stinkin' Thinkin'!

I CAN GET ON WITH MY LIFE!

I bought a new weekly planner-slash-address book today. It's going to be okay!

TODAY I WILL NOT BEOVERWHELMED! III

Okay. Jodie's getting a little impatient. She says for Kyle's sake she'd like to be able to move into Aunt Paula's house before school starts in September, and she hasn't even been able to apply for a mortgage because of the dispute. Donnie, I think, has pretty much accepted the idea that Jodie will get the house, but wants his money as soon as possible so he can move out of Mom and Dad's. Mom wants the money to fix up her house a bit. A lot of things don't work. The shower went years ago, and to fill up the bathtub we have to run a rubber tube from the bathroom faucet. The outside of the house needs work too. Little things that Dad and Donnie could easily do—like the screen on the screen door is torn. I'd do it, but believe me, I am just not handy, and besides, I simply refuse to enable them! Dad's the only one who seems in no hurry. He just wants a new rifle for deer season. Anyway, I have to be careful not to rush this thing. When I do things frantically I tend to make them a lot harder than they really are. So I've made a list in my new weekly planner-slash-address book.

And here it is:

1. Make list.
2. Call Jodie's lawyer—ask him for names of other lawyers.
3. Make list of other lawyers.
4. Call other lawyers—make appointments, discuss issues:
    a. renegotiation of easement.
    b. Aunt Paula's furniture—U-Haul.
    c. Jodie's legal bills—should Donnie pay some?
    d. U-Haul bill—should Jodie pay some?
5. Do laundry.
6. Al-Anon meeting, Unitarian Church.

I CAN TRUST MY JUDGMENT!

Too often those of us who grew up in dysfunctional homes stop trusting our judgment at an early age. "Dad wasn't drunk last night." "I never promised you I'd take you to the zoo. You must be imagining things." "Dad was not drunk this afternoon." "Don't be silly, you *like* being physically intimidated." "Dad is not drunk right now." It's no wonder we go through our adult life thinking, "I don't know what I'm doing. I'd better rely on someone else's judgment. Except, I don't trust my judgment to pick out the person whose judgment I should rely on. I'm screwed!" Well, that's just Stinkin' Thinkin'! Because today I interviewed three lawyers! I purposely made appointments with three, because if I saw only one, I'd just panic and hire that person. Anyway, I chose a lawyer today. And I chose him because he was the only one of the three lawyers who told me I should *not* be the executor. He heard the story and said immediately that having a family member as the executor was a big mistake. He said that he's seen this a million times before, and that judging from what I told him about my family and about myself, that I was the last person who should be the executor. I asked him who could do it then, and he smiled and pointed to himself. Immediately I knew that this guy was the guy, and breathed a humongous sigh of relief.

I AM NOT THE EXECUTOR!

I've called another family meeting for today. Noon again. I asked Mom to make the beans and buns again and made a little joke about it being the official traditional family probate meal, and she said she didn't know what I was talking about. So I started telling her about how she always has an official traditional food for every family event, and she got mad and thought I was criticizing her and said it wasn't true and that I was imagining things. Donnie doesn't want to go to the meeting. He said, Didn't we just have one? I told him it was important, and he said, Why can't it be later, then? I said it's a good idea to have it early in the day so Dad's sober. I think I told Dad it's a good idea to have it early in the day so Donnie's sober. Even Jodie was a little short with me. All this made me realize what a good decision I've made not to be the executor!

I AM THE EXECUTOR.

Okay. This meeting did not go as well as the first one. I think some of it might have just been due to low blood sugar. Mom had been so insulted by my "official traditional probate meal" remark that she didn't make anything and said we could all go hungry. Donnie and Jodie got on each other right away about the U-Haul bill, and Jodie started screaming and crying about the money for Kyle's swimming club, and how Kyle is the only Smalley with a chance to have a real life. Then Dad just walked out. I followed him out to the garage and told him we had to make an important decision and we couldn't do it without him. He just kind of scoffed bitterly, like he was hurt, but more angry than hurt. And I felt so guilty that I said that maybe he should be the executor. After all, Aunt Paula was his father's sister. He shook his head and said Donnie could have his vote, then got in his Olds, backed out of the garage, and drove off. Back in the house, everybody had scattered: Mom in her room, Donnie in his, and Jodie in the living room. I put on some brown 'n' serve rolls and coffee, then rounded everybody up into the kitchen. I told them about the lawyer, and how the lawyer said that it might be a bad idea for a family member to act as executor, and how I agreed. Then Donnie asked how much it would cost. And I said a hundred twenty-five an hour, and they said no.

GOD GRANT ME THE SERENITY TO ACCEPT THE THINGS I CANNOT CHANGE! II

Joanne called yesterday. I wasn't home and Mom talked to her. When Mom gave me the message, I asked her for Joanne's number, but Mom said, "She didn't leave it, she said you had it." At which point I started screaming! "Yes, I *had* it! And where do you think I *had* it, Mom?! You want a hint?! Okay, I'll give you a hint, Mom. I wrote it in something! Something that doesn't exist anymore! Something that doesn't exist because someone put it in a *washing machine!!!*" That was about fourteen hours ago, and I still haven't made an amends. That gives you some idea how angry I am! Well, I tracked down Joanne's number, and she told me she called to tell me that she and her boyfriend, Bob, were back together, that he forgave her for her fling with Ted, and actually blamed himself and his own inability to make a commitment. I told her about the whole thing with my address book-slash-weekly planner and me yelling at my Mom, and she said that the Higher Power had put the address book in the washer and that I still hadn't come to terms with it and that I had to go through the process of grieving for my address book. At this point I was mentally crossing Joanne off my list of friends, but then I realized how judgmental that was, and how that kind of Stinkin' Thinkin' is a sure sign I'm in a shame spiral. And I can't afford that today. I'm going to talk to Mr. Egeberg, Aunt Paula's neighbor, and try to renegotiate the easement. I better make an immediate amends to Mom or I'll just be no good today.

GOD GRANT ME THE COURAGE TO CHANGE THE THINGS I CAN!

As you may remember, two feet of Aunt Paula's driveway is actually on her neighbor's, Mr. Egeberg's, property, and before the bank will approve a mortgage, Mr. Egeberg must grant an easement on the two feet. So Jodie talked to Mr. Egeberg and then he sent her a letter offering to grant her the easement for three thousand dollars, which Jodie agreed to orally. Jodie wants the five of us who are splitting Aunt Paula's inheritance to split equally the cost of the easement, which everyone says is fair, except that Dad and Donnie say the three-thousand-dollar figure was agreed to without consulting them, even though Jodie's lawyer sent Donnie's lawyer several letters, which he ignored because he wasn't getting paid because he was doing it for Donnie, his old drinking buddy, as a favor. Some favor! So the family asked me, as the new executor, to try to get Mr. Egeberg to reduce the price of the easement. I felt a little funny about doing it. I mean, my sister had agreed to three thousand and shook hands. But I guess I finally figured what could be the harm if I just talked to the man and explained the situation. So yesterday I met with Mr. Egeberg, and I have to say, I had a bad feeling right away. First off, when I met him at his front door, he did not smile. As it turns out, he never did smile the whole time I was there. Also, he did not ask me inside. I thought to myself maybe the house is a mess, even though I had given him a couple days' warning, and he's just embarrassed to let me see. But I was able to look past him into the house, and I would have to say that Mr. Egeberg's is the neatest house I have ever seen. Without question! Anyway, with him standing there inside the screen door, and me out there on the front step, it felt like I wasn't going to have a lot of time, so I got right into it, explaining the whole thing like I just did, but with a lot more detail. His expression never changed; in fact, he really had no expression, so I had no idea how I was doing. Finally, I finished, and he said, "I thought we had had an agreement." And I said yes, that's right, but I explained again about Dad and Donnie feeling like they weren't consulted, and how they were hoping I could get him to change the price, and that as far as I was concerned three thousand was absolutely fine and I was willing to pay my one fifth of it, but that Donnie and Dad just would prefer if they didn't have to pay as much. And then Mr. Egeberg said, "I thought the agreement was legally binding." And that's when I think I made the mistake. Because I said, "Well, actually not, technically. Because in Minnesota, technically, I believe you would need a *written* acceptance of your offer, whereas Jodie's was only oral. Now, as far as I'm concerned, Jodie made the agreement with you and we should honor it, but I have no control over Dad and Donnie." And Mr. Egeberg said, "Ten thousand," and shut the door.

AND THE WISDOM TO KNOW THE DIFFERENCE!

I haven't discussed the Egeberg meeting with my family yet. Carl, my OA sponsor, suggested I talk to a lawyer I trust about the easement and then for sanity sake leave Minnesota as quickly as possible. I wasn't sure about the second part, but I immediately retained Arnie Juster, the lawyer who had told me it was a mistake for me to act as executor. I figured I'd just pay him myself. I showed Arnie the file of correspondence between Jodie's lawyer and Donnie's lawyer, and he agreed with my conclusions about Donnie's lawyer screwing things up by not paying attention. Then Arnie told me about twenty lawyer jokes, which were funny, but I started worrying about the time, and Arnie said not to worry, that he wasn't charging for this session, because he felt bad for me. Then we turned to the Egeberg matter. Arnie said the bad news was that it sounded like I had pissed Mr. Egeberg off. He said that was bad because Mr. Egeberg could tie this up for months, maybe longer. Arnie said the good news is that Mr. Egeberg's original offer is on paper and that my family could hold him to the three-thousand-dollar figure as long as there was no "revocation" of his offer. If it came to it, we could sue him for breech of contract. Then I asked Arnie if my conversation with Mr. Egeberg would constitute a revocation of his offer. Arnie said not really, because all I would have to do is deny what I had said. Then I told Arnie that I work a program of rigorous honesty, and I couldn't deny saying something I really said. Then Arnie asked me if a third person had overheard our conversation or if I had reason to believe that Mr. Egeberg had taped it, and I said no. And he said it was okay, I could just deny it, this would be *civil* court. Then I explained to him how I was a member of OA, Al-Anon, DA, CoDA, and ACOA and how it was just absolutely impossible for me to tell a lie. He thought about it for a few seconds and said, "That's okay." He said that Mr. Egeberg's attorney would have to assume I would lie and that was *almost* as good. I said, What if Mr. Egeberg doesn't use an attorney? And Arnie just kind of shuddered.

I AM AN HONEST PERSON. III

Arnie called me yesterday. He had phoned Mr. Egeberg to try to smooth things over, but it didn't work. Arnie was right. I had pissed the man off, and he is insisting on ten thousand for the easement. Arnie suggested we write an apologetic letter to Mr. Egeberg and try again in a week, after he's had a chance to cool down. In the meantime, he suggested I not tell my family what happened, but I said I thought they were entitled to know the truth, and Arnie sounded concerned and asked if my program of rigorous honesty included blurting out the truth even when no one had asked for it. I thought about that for a minute and said no, it doesn't include "blurting," but that sometimes withholding information can be a form of dishonesty. So Arnie agreed that it was okay for me to call a family meeting for today if I explain very carefully to everybody that *I'm* paying for Arnie and that I'm letting him handle Mr. Egeberg. So we meet at noon, in three hours. I'm going to bake a cake.

DONNIE IS THE NEW EXECUTOR.

Just one of the many things I love about my family is how they're always changing history. We met yesterday in the kitchen. When I told everyone about my conversation with Mr. Egeberg, they were horror-stricken. Jodie started crying and screaming at Donnie and Dad for having insisted that I try to renegotiate the easement. Donnie flat denied it, and then Dad said something sarcastic about Jodie recommending that an incompetent like Stuart be the executor! After that, to tell you the truth, I really can't remember who said what. I was too much in a daze. But somehow, in a matter of minutes, they all agreed to change history. No one, it seems, had asked me to try to renegotiate the easement. And they should never have allowed me to insist on being the executor. They had all known I was incompetent all along and had each said so at both of the last two meetings. Oh. And Adolf Hitler didn't start WWII. He started AA. Bill W. started WWII. I excused myself and just sat in the bathroom and cried for about twenty minutes. When I got back, everyone was on their second piece of cake, and Donnie was the new executor. He would go with Jodie to see Mr. Egeberg and they would tell Mr. Egeberg that I had not been authorized to speak on their behalf, and that the three-thousand-dollar price was fine. I tried to tell them about Arnie and his take on the situation. But they weren't really listening. Jodie and Donnie were a team now. So I guess I'd done my job. I brought the family back together. But I really could care less. I'm ashamed of my family. Especially Jodie. Screw them! Screw them all!

I AM ENTITLED TO FEEL BAD!

I wanted to make this one an "I am entitled to be angry" affirmation, but I don't feel angry, I feel bad. A little mad, but mainly bad, sad, and *had!* And that's okay. If I'm entitled to feel angry, I am entitled to feel anything I feel! I'm entitled to feel I'm unentitled, if that's how I feel. And that's how I feel. I'm leaving today. I was a fool to come; I was a fool to stay; I was a fool to let Mom put my address book in the washer. Andrea called. She had read the faxes from the last few days, and says she's worried about me. She says she's afraid I'm going to take to my bed. I told her not to worry. I'll be okay just as soon as I get out of here.

I AM NOT A VICTIM!

I've decided to stay one more day. Donnie's called a family meeting for noon. And I've decided it'll be the perfect opportunity to tell everyone off! Evidently, Donnie and Jodie's talk with Mr. Egeberg backfired. He just got madder and demanded fifteen thousand! Good for Mr. Egeberg! I know Donnie wants me to be executor again, and I'm certain everyone's just sure I'll jump at it. Well, they're in for a little surprise!

MY FAMILY IS SUING ME!

Donnie has been reading this book. And xeroxing it. And highlighting the worst stuff I've said about each member of the family. He started the meeting yesterday by distributing copies to everybody and reading aloud. I don't know why I'm even writing this. It's all over. This book is over. My life is over. Donnie said he started xeroxing after seeing the one where I said he made my skin crawl. Mom was very emotional about the April 3rd affirmation where I said I hated my parents and compared being at home unfavorably to shitting a watermelon. There was so much that Dad reacted to, I just don't know where to begin. Oh, I know. He objected to being called an alcoholic. That was the only point where I really tried to stand up for myself. "C'mon, Dad, you know you have a problem. Donnie? Mom?" And I turned to Jodie for support, but all she could stare at were the words on the page . . . "I'm ashamed of my family. Especially Jodie." Finally, she looked up at me, and I think *she* was ashamed. "C'mon, Jodie, help me out here." But she was also ashamed of being ashamed because she was going to go along with Donnie. He had a letter from his lawyer. It demanded that I pay Mr. Egeberg myself out of my share of Aunt Paula's inheritance, because I had mishandled the negotiations. And it said that if my book was published, the family would file a defamation suit. Then Jodie looked up at me and said, "Stuart, how could you write this about us?" And I said, "Jodie, you know it's all true." And she said, "But in a book?" And I said, "No. It won't be in a book."

TODAY I WILL DETACH WITH LOVE!

Joanne would probably say I chose Mallomars this time because my Higher Power knows that at a certain point they just turn on you and you can't eat any more Mallomars. As usual, this last two weeks have been a living hell. I flew home to my apartment and holed up with the Mallomars. Carl and Andrea showed up the next day, but I refused to see them. They didn't shout slogans this time. I think they realized I kind of resented it last time. Instead Carl was saying stuff like "Fuck your family!" Andrea yelled something along the same lines and tried to assure me that my family couldn't sue for me defamation. I just ignored them and after about half an hour or so they went away. But they came back the next day, and Andrea brought along a lawyer from Dell, which did get me out of bed. I just started screaming, "Get that lawyer out of this building! I'm going to look out my window, and if I don't see that lawyer on the sidewalk in two minutes, I'm going to kill myself!" And I meant it too! So Andrea and Carl rushed the lawyer down four flights of stairs, and I looked out the window and saw them run out onto the lawn toward the sidewalk. Andrea looked great! I think she'd lost another thirty pounds. Carl looked good too. As they hit the sidewalk, Andrea and Carl looked up to my window and we made eye contact. Their looks of concern just made me feel worse about myself and I turned from the window and went back to bed. They were back the next day, and the next. Finally, on the fifth day, Carl just said, "Okay, Stuart, we've had it. We clearly are powerless over this, and that makes us feel very sad. But we're going to have to detach, Stuart, because this is driving us crazy. Andrea and I are going fishing for a week. You're going to have to get out of this hole yourself. We love you, Stuart. Good luck." They were detaching with love. I opened a box of Mallomars and thought about that. Detaching with love. One of the basic tenets of Al-Anon, maybe *the* basic tenet. How many times had I explained to new Al-Anon members the needless state of inner turmoil we keep ourselves in when we become involved in all the affairs of our alcoholic? How many times have I talked about the importance of removing our need to control what we can't control? Then why did I fail so miserably when it came to detaching from my family? Why had I been a classic boob? *The* classic boob. And this book. Was it loving to write about them? I looked back at what I had written and decided that a lot of it was. A lot of it wasn't. And what did that matter? Do I have the right to tell my story if it's also their story? I don't mean legal right, I could care less about that. Didn't I tell them I was doing this? And besides, haven't they treated me like something on their shoe? But then again . . . And I was back in the same loop. Two weeks of lying in bed, eating Mallomars, thinking the same set of thoughts over and over again. And finally, the Mallomars just turned on me. I couldn't stand it anymore. And I realized I had to detach. I had to detach with love *from my own sick thoughts*. And when Andrea and Carl showed up yesterday with sunburns and a stringer of bass, we cooked 'em up and talked about a million other things.

TODAY I DECLARE EMOTIONAL INDEPENDENCE FROM MY FAMILY!!

I stole this one from Rokelle Lerner's *Daily Affirmations for ACOA,* but I don't think she'd mind. If she does, Rokelle, I owe you an amends. Anyway, declaring emotional independence is a scary thing. It basically means that you have decided to become an adult, with your own sets of values and goals. Which is okay! In fact, it's absolutely necessary! My Critical Inner Voice is telling me to feel guilty. But there's nothing to feel guilty about! Because the alternative is what you saw in Minnesota: living your life in total frustration and resentment. And I refuse to do that! So, Mom and Dad, Donnie, and Jodie, I love you (even though you treated me like something on the bottom of your shoe), but today I declare my emotional independence from you! There. I feel like Patrick Henry at his first Al-Anon meeting. Give me liberty, One Day at a Time! (By the way, the analogy is not that farfetched. Evidently, King George was a rage-aholic in total denial!)

I DON'T HAVE TO DECIDE TODAY. II

I am going to continue writing this book, even though my family is dead set against it. Well, I can write today, and if I want to, write tomorrow, and so on. And if at the end of the year, *I* decide that it would be an invasion of their privacy for me to publish this book, then I won't. Obviously, if you're reading this, dear reader, then I decided to publish. If you're not reading this . . . well, then whatever I say here . . . Okay, if you're not reading this, then you wouldn't be . . . Okay, I'm very confused.

TODAY I WILL THINK CLEARLY, AND NOT BE CONFUSED OR GET CONFUSED, WHICHEVER!

Many of us who have addictive attitudes get confused at the drop of a hat. And that makes a lot of sense, if you think about it. Because we don't really know ourselves. And sometimes when we get into recovery, we can experience even greater confusion. We codependents, who are used to *re*-acting to the people and situations around us, now have to learn to *act* for ourselves, and feel *our own* feelings, and decide what *we* want out of life. Even the program itself can be confusing. Take some of the slogans. "Let go, and let God." Okay. Good advice. Sometimes we can obsess about something to the point where we should just let go. *But* "Awareness, Acceptance, Action," the 3 *A*'s. Sometimes you have to know when to "take the action" or "an" action, or whatever. So here's my confusion. When do I *let go?* And when do I *take an action?* For me it all boils down to the last line of the Serenity Prayer:

> God grant me the serenity
> To accept the things I cannot change.
> Courage to change the things I can,
> *And wisdom to know the difference.*

Well, thank you very much! If I had the wisdom to know the difference, you would see one serene, courageous dude here! But anyway, it's okay. It's Okay! Because it's a process. And if I work the process, every day I will get a little wiser, a little more courageous, and a little more serene. And you know what? I have a confession. When I started this affirmation, I was scared to death that I would get confused while doing it. And I didn't! So you see, it works! . . . Whatever "it" is. . . .

I DON'T HAVE TO MOTHER, MANAGE, OR MANIPULATE—THE THREE *M*'S!!!

Carl suggested that I go to more Al-Anon meetings, since my last crisis was really an Al-Anon slip. Which reminds me about a joke a friend of mine in AA once told me: "Did you hear about the Al-Anon member who had a slip? He had a moment of compassion." Which I didn't think was very funny. At least at the time, because I was in early recovery and didn't have much of a sense of humor about the whole thing. I think my answer was, "Did you hear about the alcoholic who had a slip? He got drunk and hit his kid. Ha, ha." But now I am able to laugh about this stuff. And when I went to yesterday's meeting, I was struck with how much laughter you hear in the rooms. (Actually, I've been to a few open AA meetings, and they laugh about twice as much as we do. Talk about unfair!) Anyway, at yesterday's meeting, Steve, whose wife is an alcoholic, shared the three *M*'s—I don't have to *Mother*, *Manage*, or *Manipulate*! And everyone laughed, because we have the three *A*'s (Awareness, Acceptance, Action), the three *C*'s (didn't Cause it, can't Control it, can't Cure it), the new three *C*'s (Cope, Change, and Celebrate) and now the three *M*'s! What's next? The three *Z*'s? See how much fun you can have when you maintain your sense of humor? Oh, I think I got the three *Z*'s: I will catch my three *Z*'s. You know, because it's important for us codependents to get our sleep!!!

TODAY I WILL LAUGH—AT LEAST ONCE!

You know what? Yesterday's affirmation is one of my favorites! Because I made myself laugh! I know it's a dumb joke. But that's okay! The three *Z*'s. I tried that at an Al-Anon meeting yesterday and to tell you the truth, only one person laughed—Steve, who thought of the three *M*'s, and I think that's just because he's really into thinking about different combinations of "the three . . . you know, whatevers." Anyway, I just think it's so important to see the humor in your life. When I lived with Dale, my rage-aholic ex, I don't think I laughed once. But laughter is such a release! It's like the mind and the soul having sex! Not with each other . . . But, gee, I'm having a déjà vu. This is the strangest feeling. I feel like I've been here before, sitting in my living room, talking into my tape recorder. Well, of course, I have; I've been doing this for six months. Anyway, I'm sorry. . . . I don't know where I am.

I AM REPEATING MYSELF.

I realize now why I was having a déjà vu yesterday. My affirmation was almost *exactly* the same as my March 21st affirmation. In fact, it's almost word for word. But that's okay! Maybe I *needed* to say the same thing twice exactly the same way. Or maybe I'm in a rut. Which is okay! Anyway, it's important to laugh. Okay, now I've said that three times. So I'll stop now.

TODAY I WILL LEARN SOMETHING!

What a powerful idea! Today I will learn something! Very often we can get into ruts, like I did, and tend to create an ever smaller world for ourselves, thinking more and more about less and less. Geez, did I say that? That's not bad! Thinking more and more about less and less. Sometimes just the act of learning about something can open up a whole new universe and help us to see the infiniteness of life. Infiniteness of life. Did I say that? Anyway, you know what I mean. So today I have decided to expand my universe. Next week I will fly to Baltimore to spend four days at the National Shame Conference!

I Don't Have to Be an Anorexic Spender!

I woke up yesterday in a panic. I was thinking, Am I crazy, I don't have the money to go to the National Shame Conference! I might have to return my book advance; I was fired from my job; and I'm probably going to lose money on the Aunt Paula thing! What on earth am I thinking about paying for a plane ticket and hotel, let alone the registration fee for the conference, which is close to three hundred bucks! I immediately got myself to a DA (Debtors Anonymous) meeting and shared. And guess who was at the meeting? Joanne. She was upset because she and Bob had broken up again. Anyway, Joanne and I went out for coffee, and she was really helpful. She knows my history and reminded me of my tendency not to spend money on myself. (Remember the cardboard belt?) She called this anorexic spending. Which is very appropriate, even though I think it's not a program term, but one that Joanne made up herself, because she used to have an eating disorder. (She was bulimic, which I've actually heard her joke about, which I think is very healthy. She said she was bulimic because she wanted to be sexy and yet eat constantly!) Anyway, Joanne said that I had a spiritual problem, which I think I agree with. She told me I don't trust the Higher Power to provide enough for me and that's why I was afraid to spend on myself. So, for today, I have decided to trust H.P. and fly to Baltimore next week for the National Shame Conference!

THE HIGHER POWER WILL PROVIDE FOR ME!

I decided to share what Joanne told me at an Al-Anon meeting. And guess what? Steve, whose wife is an alcoholic in early recovery, came up to me afterward and suggested we go for coffee. Well, to make a long story short, Steve said he needed to get away from his wife for a week, because he would like to kill her, and he said he felt ashamed of that because he knows she has a disease, but he'd still just like to kill her. So anyway, he said he'd like to go to the National Shame Conference and that maybe he could drive us both, you know, to keep expenses down. And I said, great, maybe we could even share a hotel room. And then he said the oddest thing, which was, "I just want you to know, I'm not gay." And I said, "Of course not, you have a wife and children." And he said, "I know, but that doesn't necessarily mean anything. I just want you to know I'm doing this because I've listened to you share and I think you're a good person and I need to get away from my wife for a few days." And I said, "I know." And he said, "So I just want you to know at the outset, I'm not gay." That's when I realized that he was telling me this because he was assuming that *I* was gay. Well, then I told him— Um, fill 'er up . . . Um, unleaded regular, I think, I don't know, it's his car. . . . Well, I think he just went to the rest room, maybe we should just wait. . . . Wait a minute, I see something here. Okay, "use only unleaded regular," so I guess . . . right, right. . . . Anyway, we're on our way to the National Shame Conference!!

I Am a Good Listener!

Sometimes those of us with addictive attitudes don't listen. Sometimes we're so busy controlling other people's lives, we just expect people to listen to us, and as a result we don't hear what other people have to say. Or sometimes we hear what they have to say, for about ten seconds, and then spend the next hour solving their problems for them, when all they wanted was someone to vent to. In fact, right now I feel like I'm just talking and not listening, so I'm going to pause a little and listen to my Higher Power tell me what to say next. . . . Okay. My Higher Power suggested I talk about Steve, who I listened to yesterday for about sixteen hours. He had a tremendous amount to get off his chest, and I resisted the urge to get in there and tell him what to do. For instance, he really should see a marriage counselor. But I didn't tell him that outright, because in Al-Anon we're not supposed to give advice as such. At least nothing as concrete as that. Anyway, I did tell him that maybe he and his wife could talk to a third, objective person, so I guess in a way I did make that suggestion without it coming in the form of advice. The point is Steve just *hates* his wife. And I think he feels guilty about it, because I think Steve feels guilty about just about everything. Which reminds me of me. Anyway, Steve's wife has been sober about a year, and Steve didn't really start hating her until about six months ago. I think a lot of it has to do with her behavior while she was drinking. She would yell at him and tell him he was an asshole and a lousy father, and Steve would buy into it and think he was working too hard at work and not spending enough time at home, even though he hated it at home, and he'd feel guilty. Steve had no idea she was an alcoholic; she hid her drinking, even though she drank about a quart of vodka a day. Steve just thought she was going crazy and he blamed himself. He thought he was such a bad husband that he was driving his wife crazy! Then one day he got a call to pick up his wife at the emergency room. She had taken some Valium along with the booze and passed out. They rushed her to the hospital, where they pumped her stomach. Steve was horrified when he saw her on the gurney, her face was all bruised from the fall. But Steve also was relieved. He said he realized then that his wife had a real problem, that it was *her* fault, and that maybe he wasn't to blame. She went into rehab the next day, and Steve said he thought all his problems were over. . . . Fill 'er up, unleaded regular . . . Um, I don't know . . . maybe you should ask, oh there he is . . . Steve, should he check the oil? . . . Well, gotta go. Point is . . . listen.

D.ON'T E.VEN (K)N.OW I. A.M L.YING.

That's Steve's. Even though he's been in the program only a year, he knows every slogan. He kind of collects them. That's his sense of humor. Which is great, which is why Steve is so successful in his work. He's in advertising. He writes commercials, mainly funny ones. I mean, we have been laughing so hard. Mainly at how miserable his life is. Steve hasn't had sex in six months. I think that's one of the main reasons he's mad at his wife. Evidently, since she got out of rehab, she has not initiated sex once. Which, according to her, is very common. Steve said that when she got out of rehab, he thought the problem had been solved. He Didn't Even (K)Now He . . . well, he was in denial. Anyway, I think Steve is thinking he's going to get divorced, but he loves his kids. So he's depressed. I think if he didn't have a sense of humor, he'd be almost comatose. For instance, yesterday Steve told me he's so horny that he looks at practically every woman and imagines having sex with her. He said, "I think I'm a lesbian trapped inside a man's body!" I've heard some people say that humor can be a defense which prevents you from sharing your real feelings. Maybe that's true. But I think Steve's sense of humor keeps him sane, and it certainly hasn't prevented me from getting to know him. And though in many ways we couldn't be two more different human beings, I feel we have a lot in common, and he makes me feel more like a human being. Well, anyway, tonight we get to Baltimore, and both of us have vowed to have a great time at the National Shame Conference!!

I AM SO ASHAMED!

I am in Baltimore, sitting in my hotel room at the National Shame Conference, which is being held here at the Marriott. Steve has gone down to breakfast and registration, but I needed to sit down and write this. I feel so ashamed. Last night as I was trying to fall asleep, a thought hit me. How could I write about Steve without even asking him for permission? I lay awake all night. Am I crazy? Didn't I learn anything from the experience with my family? I wanted to go over to Steve's bed and wake him up and make an amends. Then I realized I should really make an amends to everybody. Joanne. I've never told her about the book. And the Knoblauchs. Even Ted, my sex addict boss who fired me. I have no business writing this book! I have no business writing about other people! This should be what I thought it was going to be—a simple daily affirmation book. You know, "I am God's creation!" kind of thing. I mean, what have I done? I have to call Andrea and tell her this has been a huge mistake; I'll give her back the advance! With interest! I'll burn the book! I have a copy with me. Okay, I am going to burn the book and *then* call everybody. Okay. I think I'm in a shame spiral. Which is okay. It's *my* shame spiral and I'm owning it. But why is this happening? Could it be because I am here at the National Shame Conference? I mean, when we arrived last night, I met some of the people here. Family therapists, drug rehab counselors, employment assistance program managers, doctors, various experts—all professionals in the recovery community. I feel like I'm not entitled to be at the National Shame Conference!

TODAY I WILL KNOW, I WILL LOVE, I WILL FEEL!

This conference is a miracle! It's as if everybody is talking about me! The first speaker spoke on how our three basic powers (to know, to love, to feel) are shamed early in life. And believe me, it's true. My parents always thought we were idiots, and were candid enough to tell us. At every possible opportunity! And just in case we actually perceived something, they let us know we were crazy: "Didn't Dad fall down the basement stairs last night and not move when we tried to pick him up?" "What are you talking about!? He was just sleeping." And feelings? Please! And love? Please, *please!!* Steve and I stayed up last night and talked about this stuff. Steve told me his mother always told him he was a genius, and she would brag about him to all her friends. What I would have given for that! But Steve says he never really believed it. And every time he achieved anything, he thought he was fooling everyone. And the more he achieved, the bigger the imposter he thought he was. I told Steve I felt like an imposter too, and then I told him about the book, and how I felt I had violated his privacy, and how I wanted to burn the book. So Steve sat down and *read the book!* I couldn't stand being in the room, so I went down to the lobby and wandered into the cocktail lounge, where this woman in a sequined gown was singing "Just the Way You Are." There were about three other people in this big room, and when I ordered a club soda, I could tell that the waitress was upset. She told me she hates these recovery conferences. Terrible for business. Anyway, I listened to the song, and I started thinking how weird the lyrics are. "Don't go changin' . . ." I started thinking, What if the other person *wants* to change? Then she sang "Stand by Your Man," which suddenly dawned on me as the ultimate codependent anthem. Until, that is, she sang "Ain't No Mountain High Enough," you know, "to keep me from you." And I thought, I know how to pack the place during the conference. Just advertise "Alcohol-free codependent song night." Anyway, this distracted me for a good hour; I had three club sodas, left a nice tip, and walked out as she went into "Set Me Free, Why Don't You, Babe?" I went upstairs, and Steve was just about to the end of June. I waited in the bathroom till he yelled he was finished. I walked into the room, and Steve hugged me. He said he thought I was the most honest person he had ever met, and that he would be proud to have me write about him in the book. But he said he wanted me to change his name, because he didn't want to embarrass his wife, and he thought he'd be able to be more honest if he knew his name wasn't being used. So from now on Steve's name will be . . . Steve! And I'll go back and change all the Steve's to Steve. So I guess, as far as you're concerned, he was always Steve. Anyway, he's Steve.

TODAY I WILL BE MY TRUE SELF, BECAUSE MY TRUE SELF IS GOOD ENOUGH!!

I love this conference! Even though I only slept four hours (Steve and I stayed up till three talking to these two nurses from Philadelphia who work in a rehab), I feel so energized! And I know why! We spend so much energy being our false selves, hiding, carrying secrets, pretending to be what we're not, that when we let our true selves out, we . . . well, we have a lot of energy! (I didn't say we get articulate. But that's okay!) Tomorrow is the last day of the conference, and on the one hand I don't want to leave, and on the other I can't wait to get back to my real life, whatever that is, and apply what I've learned here. Anyway, it's about seven in the morning, and I'm going to head down for breakfast. Steve must already be down there, because he's not here and his bed is made. . . . That's odd. Why did he make his bed? The maid makes the bed. Anyway, I'm looking forward to this morning's seminar on intimacy!

INFATUATION IS GREAT! BUT I WILL RECOGNIZE IT FOR WHAT IT IS!

Okay. I'm only writing about this because Steve said it was okay. Steve says it's a good thing he went to the intimacy seminar with Donna (the nurse he slept with two nights ago and last night), because he thought he was in love with her. The speaker said a lot of great things, but the thing that hit Steve was, "Healthy people don't say 'I love you' during infatuation." Which Steve later told me he did. Actually, I think he said it during . . . well, I can't believe I'm talking about this. Anyway, I sat with Steve and Donna at lunch. And, boy, they are infatuated with each other! They couldn't stop looking at each other or touching each other. Which is terrific. Except that Steve is married. Which Donna knows. I mean, I think they know practically everything about each other, which is I guess what happens when you fall in . . . infatuation at the National Shame Conference. Anyway, today's the last day of the conference, and Steve doesn't know what to do. I know I'm not supposed to give advice, but I did kind of suggest that maybe he should fly home and go to a marriage counselor with his wife and I could drive his car back myself. Steve was thinking something more on the lines of quitting his job and starting up a new life in the Bahamas with Donna. Donna, whom I really like, said she doesn't want to be a home-wrecker and that she thought the speaker at the intimacy seminar was right, that they should recognize the infatuation for what it is—a chemical attraction to someone else, and that Steve shouldn't do anything rash, and he should remember that he is now basically temporarily insane and that he should remember he hadn't had sex in six months. And then they went up to her room. I'm not sure what's going to happen, or even how I'm getting home, because I didn't really get to talk to them the rest of the day. But I did see them holding hands in the Overcoming Perfectionism seminar.

THIS TOO SHALL PASS. II

We're near Pittsburgh. I've been doing most of the driving, because Steve's been crying a lot. Mainly, it's about his kids. He keeps looking at their pictures and crying. In fact, we've had to stop a lot so Steve can call either his kids or call Donna. Steve says he feels incredibly guilty, which is making him even angrier at his wife and her drinking. I mentioned perhaps forgiving her, and Steve said he'd like to hitch her to a huge grinding wheel and lash her with a whip as she went round and round, and do that for two years, which is how long she had been drinking excessively and verbally abusing him. *Then* and only then would he *consider* forgiving her. Then he went into how wonderful Donna is and how she understands what he's been through because her ex-husband is an alcoholic. And how beautiful she is, which . . . I mean she's pretty. And how young she is. And now I'm thinking, Oh boy, I wonder who to bet on: the young pretty nurse who understands him, or the old wife he wants to hitch to a grindstone? Then he starts talking about his kids and how the last thing he wants to do is abandon his kids in any way. And then he starts crying. And I tell him, "This too shall pass." And it worked only very marginally.

I AM NOT RESPONSIBLE FOR HOW OTHER PEOPLE FEEL!

Okay. The last day or so has not been fun. Steve is a wreck, and of course, I have been trying to cheer him up and make him see that things will get better and he'll be less confused, and things will become clearer to him, and so on. But it seemed like the more we talked, the worse he felt, and he even got mad at me at one point and threw my own bottoms (taking to my bed) in my face. And I mean in an angry, inappropriate way. So I pulled the car over at the next rest stop, went into the bathroom, and looked in that mirror and said, "I am not responsible for how other people feel." So I got back in the car and decided I wasn't going to talk, so I turned on the radio and guess what came on? "Stand by Your Man." And I started to laugh and Steve asked me what I was laughing at and I told him and he started to laugh. And then he made his amends and we started listening to music and having a great time. So it just shows you. Once I decided I wasn't responsible for cheering Steve up, I cheered Steve up. And me too! God, I love this program!

I AM STEVE'S SPONSOR.

The last leg of our trip was great. Steve got ahold of himself, and as we got closer to home, I kept urging him to see a marriage counselor or couples therapist or whatever they call themselves now. Steve thinks his wife will freak out if he brings it up, but I said that's okay. It's better than not bringing it up. But I told him I didn't mean he should tell his wife about Donna. And Steve said, "I think I owe it to her." And I said, "No, don't!" And he said, "No, I have to make an amends to her." And I said, "No, no!! You don't have to! The Ninth Step is 'Make direct amends to such people wherever possible, *except when to do so would injure them* or others.' And telling your wife would injure her." And Steve said, "No, I couldn't live with myself if I don't tell her." Then Steve started laughing. He said he was yanking my chain! Just before Steve dropped me off at home, he asked me to be his sponsor. In Al-Anon, or any twelve-step program, one of the first things they tell you to do is get a sponsor, someone who you can call and talk through what's going on with you. Someone whom you respect, someone who sounds good and wise at the meetings. I was the first person Steve had ever asked to be his sponsor. And in the four years I had been in the program, Steve was the first person who had asked me to sponsor them. I started to think about the awesome responsibility. And of how much Carl, my OA sponsor, had helped me. (And then immediately felt guilty because I hadn't called him in two weeks!) And I asked Steve why in the world he asked me, and Steve said that basically it was very simple. He could be his true self with me. And he could be totally honest, and around me he felt he could know and love and feel. So said I would be his sponsor and started to cry and Steve said he would immediately withdraw his request if I continued to cry.

THE HIGHER POWER
WILL PROVIDE FOR ME. II

My first day back home and I made a lot of phone calls. Called all my sponsors and told them I was now a sponsor myself and asked them all for advice. Carl said his advice was not to give advice, but to listen and be there and let Steve find his own answers. I said I already knew that, and Carl said that's why I'm going to be a great sponsor. Steve called and said that he was going to call a couple marriage counselors to ask them for advice on how to broach the subject with his wife. I agreed that that was a good action to take and then I made what I think is a very good point, which is that Steve could use the marriage counselors' answers as a way of assessing them. And Steve said that was a good point. So I think my first day as a sponsor has been very successful, and I don't mean to be grandiose. Anyway, then I called Joanne. And guess what? She and Bob are back together! And they have gone in on a lake house in Wisconsin with some of Bob's friends from the commodities exchange, and Joanne invited me to spend a couple days up there. So here I am. No job, no money, and I'm looking for my swimsuit and fishing rod, packing for a few days in the country!

I HAVE THE RIGHT TO HAVE A GREAT DAY, ALTHOUGH I WON'T GET MY EXPECTATIONS TOO HIGH!

I just packed a lunch for the bus ride up to Joanne and Bob's lake house. I've got the stereo blasting, and I'm having a great time. I am *really* looking forward to this little side trip, so much so that I'm a little worried that I'm creating unrealistic expectations. Because expectations are just set-ups for disappointment. How many times have I created this image of what's going to happen, only to find . . . Oh, screw it! I'm going to have a great time!

TODAY I WILL BE OPEN TO THE WONDERMENT OF THIS WORLD!

This is just a spectacular place! A large, four-bedroom house! A beautiful two-acre lawn. And, of course, the lake! Joanne and Bob seemed distracted yesterday, so I took this little rowboat out with my fishing gear, and you know what? I never even put my line out. The sky was blue and the sun beating down and the water was lapping against the side of the boat. I drifted into some reeds and watched a couple dragonflies flitting about. How can there not be a Higher Power? I thought. Then I heard Joanne in the distance shouting for me. It was Steve. By the time I got to the phone, he really couldn't talk, but I think he had talked to a few marriage counselors. I'll give him a call later this morning. But first I'm going to go to this beautiful vegetable garden and do some weeding. They've got tomatoes, and beets, and green beans, and herbs, and lettuce, and Swiss chard, and even broccoli. How can there not be a Higher Power? Well, I gotta get out there before it gets hot, so— Yeah? . . . Steve? . . . Tell him I'll be right there!

TODAY I CAN BE GRATEFUL THAT I AM NOT IN A HORRIBLE RELATIONSHIP!

Holy moly! Thank God this is a big house. Joanne and Bob were screaming at each other all day. I think it has to do with who's coming up for the weekend. Specifically, Bob's old girlfriend, Sharon, who is now the girlfriend of Bob's best friend, Frank, who's one of the people that went in on the house. Joanne doesn't believe Bob that Frank and Sharon just got together and that Bob didn't purposely go in on a house with his old girlfriend. Bob says he's sick of Joanne's jealousy . . . and well, I shouldn't be talking about this. I've just been overhearing it. I can't help it, they've been screaming, but I shouldn't talk about something that wasn't directly told to me. Also, I have decided to go back and change Joanne's name to Joanne and Bob's name to Bob. (From now on, just assume the name you're reading is not really the name of the person. Except me. I am Stuart. And Andrea is really Andrea, and so are Donnie and . . . well, anyway, just understand that I'm doing the best I can to protect people's privacy.) Which reminds me, Steve did call—I spent about an hour on the phone, and he is in a living hell. Basically, he hates his wife, can barely look at her at home, is pining for Donna, whom he calls about three times a day, and just about cries every time he even sees the kids, let alone tucks them in and watches them sleep. He can't concentrate at work and he's having headaches. He's made some progress on the marriage counselor front, but he's wondering if he really wants to go, if he really wants to save his marriage. He reminded me of a line we heard at the Intimacy seminar at the Shame Conference. "We are more alone with someone who we are not connected with than we are by ourselves." I said maybe going to the marriage counselor will help him and his wife get connected again. There was this long pause. He said that it's been so long, he can't believe they ever really were truly connected. He sounded so lonely.

JOANNE AND BOB BROKE UP.

I had told myself I'd get up really early in the country, but I spent most of the night comforting Joanne, and didn't wake up until eleven. I'm sitting here in the garden, because, frankly, I just had to get away from her. Bob drove back to the city, so it's just the two of us until the weekend, when like six other people are coming, and I guess now both of us will have to leave. This is so . . . Oh God, here she comes. . . . Well, at least she's not crying. . . . Phone? . . . Steve? Okay, I'm coming.

TODAY I WILL REMEMBER THAT ALCOHOLISM IS A CUNNING, BAFFLING, POWERFUL DISEASE! II

I spent most of yesterday on the phone with Steve, which is just as well, because Joanne was just in a funk, and whenever I'd try to talk to her, she'd just start crying. Steve spoke to four different marriage counselors, asking each the same question: How would you suggest I broach the subject of going to a marriage counselor to my wife? And there were four radically different answers. The worst one, I thought, was that Steve should tell his wife that he was going to counseling for individual help, and that the therapist felt he couldn't deal with Steve unless he could talk to her. In other words, trick her into therapy, which I thought was just a little dishonest. The therapist who sounded the best to me was a woman named, ironically, Dr. Best. Her response to Steve's question was a simple, "Is your wife aware that there's a problem?" Steve said yes, and they talked awhile over the phone. When Steve told Dr. Best that his wife was a recovering alcoholic, she laughed and said, "Oh." Steve said, "Oh?" and Dr. Best said that the marriage and the alcoholism had to be dealt with together. "It's a cunning, baffling, powerful disease," said Dr. Best. When I heard that, I broke my advice rule and told Steve that Dr. Best sounded great and he should go with her. But Steve said he had already made the same decision, so in a way I felt good that he had found the same answer himself, but I also had this odd thought that I had used my one advice chip at the wrong time. Which is a sick thought. Anyway, Steve scheduled a session for himself and his wife with Dr. Best. And I said, "You never said what Dr. Best said about broaching the idea to your wife." And Steve said Dr. Best said, "Find a moment when you're even-keeled and just tell her you feel there are some problems and that you think it might help to talk to an objective third person." And I'm thinking, Why didn't I say that?

I AM THE ONLY ONE IN CONTROL OF MY LIFE!

Joanne drove me back to the city yesterday, and, of course, we did nothing but talk about her and Bob. A big part of the whole mess is Bob's inability to commit, but I told her to keep the focus on herself. Joanne admitted that she plays a big role in the thing, and that she doesn't even know if Bob's the right person for her. In fact, right now, she doesn't know much of anything. She doesn't know if she loves Bob; she doubts her own ability to make decisions for herself; she's just confused. Like they said at the shame conference, we have three basic powers: to know, to feel, and to love, and those of us in the grip of this disease lose those powers. I asked her how she could be so upset with Bob's inability to commit when she didn't know if she wanted to commit to him. Then I realized how stupid I sounded and Joanne said something about the abyss of not being in a relationship and the prison of being in one. And I thought about the prison I had been in with my rage-aholic ex, Dale. And it occurred to me how bad I was feeling and how I had spent five days in the country and spent maybe an hour on the lake. And I remembered that I am not responsible for how other people feel. But I am responsible for how I feel. So I asked Joanne to pull over at the next rest stop. And I went into the bathroom and looked in that mirror and said, "I am not responsible for how other people feel." And when I got back in the car, I decided I was not going to talk and turned on the radio, and guess what was on? Tom Jones singing "Please Release Me." And I laughed and tried to explain my theory about how most love songs are just sick codependent songs, and Joanne just looked at me.

TODAY I WILL DO SOMETHING FOR MYSELF!

Very often we forget the value of actually saying to ourselves, "Hey, I'm going to do something for *me*." Well, it's about seven in the morning, and it's about eighty-five out already. It's going to be a hot one! So, since I've gotten a little taste for the lake life, I am packing a lunch, going down to Lake Michigan, and parking my carcass in a lawn chair with a good book, *Healing the Shame That Binds You* by John Bradshaw.

I CAN SET GOALS!

Reading Bradshaw's book yesterday was incredibly inspiring. Although it was sometimes painful to relive past abuses and degradations, the book left me very hopeful. And among other things it reminded me how important a book can be to people, and so, dear reader, I hope you're getting a lot out of this book and that it's not a horrible disappointment. The shame conference and Bradshaw's book have made me realize what a large role toxic shame has played in all aspects of my life. And it hit me that shame played a large role in the demise of my cable TV show, *Daily Affirmations with Stuart Smalley.* You see, every time I did a bad show, I would feel ashamed. And I was so afraid of having that terrible feeling of shame that I put incredible pressure on myself to do perfect shows, which no one can do. And when I did do a good show, I would get all grandiose, thinking I'm so great because I helped people, and next thing you knew, I was feeling ashamed of my grandiosity. And I think those feelings of shame were what led me to yell at Roz Weinman, the woman who had power over my show, and then who subsequently canceled it. Well, I think I've grown since then, and if I haven't, I think I can change. I have decided to try to get my show back! I have set a goal!

I WILL NOT BLOCK MYSELF FROM TAKING ACTION!

How often do we allow fear to block us from taking steps toward achieving our goals? A lot! I think I've wanted to get my daily affirmations cable show back for a long time, but I've been afraid to admit it. I think I've been afraid that if I tried to get it back, I'd fail, and that would prove I'd never get it back. In other words, at least by not trying to get it back, getting it back would always exist as a vague possibility. Wow! It's amazing how you figure things out sometimes just because you force yourself to talk about them or write them down. "Today I will start a journal" would be a good affirmation. I think I'll use that one soon, because it's good advice. Anyway, I also think I've been afraid to go back to talk to Roz Weinman. Roz is head of programming at the local public access channel, and the last time I saw her I was screaming at her, because she had just canceled my show. I think if you know anything about me by now it's that I try to make immediate amends, and it's been about nine months since that last meeting, in which I called her a dysfunctional bitch, which she is, or was—I don't know, she might have changed. Anyway, it was still uncalled for, and I guess I do owe Roz an amends. I'm just afraid of how she will react. But I should just let go of the result, which is what I told Steve. Which reminds me. Speaking of not letting fear block you from taking action, Steve finally told his wife he wanted to see a marriage counselor. And you know what? She was relieved! She wanted to see one too. So if you've been wanting to do something, but have been afraid to, what the hell, just do it!

FORGIVING IS FOR-GETTING!

I tried to call Roz yesterday to arrange a meeting to make an amends. I just couldn't do it. And I realized why. I just couldn't forgive her. So I went to an Al-Anon meeting and shared about it, and Debbi, this wonderful nineteen-year-old girl, said the neatest slogan. "Forgiving is for getting." Because when you for*give* you *get* . . . something, whatever. The point is holding on to resentments only hurts you and not the person you are resentful toward. Roz Weinman doesn't care that my stomach turns sour every time I think of her, but I sure do. So, Roz, I forgive you. There. I feel much better!

ROZ WEINMAN IS A HORRIBLE, NASTY, DYSFUNCTIONAL BITCH!

I don't want to get into a whole history here, but suffice it to say, we never got along and she always hated my daily affirmations show. Which is okay. She's entitled to her opinion. I'm also entitled to my opinion, which is that she is a grandiose, shame-based overeater, sick in her own disease! . . . Not to take her inventory. A little history, I guess, is necessary. Originally, when I started my cable show, it was on at twelve noon. And I would get letters from people thanking me for giving them a chance to focus on themselves during their lunch hour. Then Roz was named head of the station, and the first thing she did was move my show to 2:45 A.M. and moved a hair transplant infomercial into my noontime slot. I was very angry, which is okay—I'm entitled to get angry—but I did an inappropriate thing and talked about her on the air, calling her a diseased person, and she, of course, canceled my show, which I have to take ultimate responsibility for, because I acted out on my anger, which was stupid and self-destructive. But we all make mistakes, and I forgive myself for my mistake. So yesterday, I called Roz up, which took some courage, and asked if I could take her to coffee to make an amends, and she said no. She said I could come to her office, and she'd give me five minutes. When I got there, she kept me waiting for about two and a half hours, and when I finally got into her office, she just showed me a file full of letters from viewers thanking her for yanking my show. Then she grinned and asked me for my amends. I told her I was sorry I had called her a diseased person on the air, and then I couldn't help myself and said I should have called her a horrible, nasty, dysfunctional bitch. Then I ran out of the room, and cried in the elevator. All I could think on the way down, and the thought cannot get out of my mind is: why on God's earth did I have to say that? Because now I owe this horrible, nasty, dysfunctional bitch another amends.

THE HIGHER POWER WILL PROVIDE FOR ME. III

After doing yesterday's affirmation, I was at a new low. Actually saying aloud the thought that I owe Roz Weinman another amends sent me back to bed with a box of Hydrox. For some reason the convenience store down the block didn't have Oreos. Anyway, I was dangerously close to another bottom . . . when Joanne called. She and Bob talked, and since they've broken up, they have decided to give me their share in the country house! Bob, who paid for it, has decided to spend August working in the city, and Joanne doesn't feel she could stay at a house full of Bob's friends. And you know what? This is just what I need. Some time in the country to think and reflect and commune with nature. Joanne said the Higher Power knew that's what I needed, and that's why Roz Weinman acted the way she did, because if Roz had given me my old show back, I couldn't use the country house. I said making Roz Weinman a horrible, nasty, dysfunctional bitch all so I can spend a month in the country seemed like an inefficient use of H.P.'s will, and Joanne accused me of not being spiritual. Anyway, I am spiritual, and I am very grateful that for the month of August anyway, Stuart is going to be a country squire!

TODAY I REFUSE TO PLACE BLAME!

Well, I'm packing. And every time I pack for a long adventure like this one, I end up getting everything out and wind up seeing my old fifty-seven-inch-waist pants. And I think how lucky I am. Lucky to be a gratefully recovering overeater, lucky to be healthy and alive! But even as I'm packing, with the music blaring from my stereo, I am sad. For Steve. And for his wife. They went to the marriage counselor yesterday, and Steve had hoped it would be a big relief. But it wasn't. At one point, early in the session, the marriage counselor asked Steve to tell his wife what it was like when she was drinking. Steve did and he cried and told how awful it was. But Steve's wife just got angry. And she accused him of arranging the marriage counseling session just to give himself a chance to blame her. And she said how terrible and humiliating and awful it had been while she was drinking, and how hard she was trying to forgive herself and to be a good mother and how the last thing she needed was Steve blaming her. And then she blamed Steve for being selfish and angry and an asshole. And I'm sitting here thinking about blame, and about how lonely blame makes you feel, even—or maybe especially—when the person you're blaming is yourself.

I LIKE TO COOK!

This country house is so different now, filled as it is with people having a good time! Dirk picked me up at the bus station. He works with Bob on the commodities exchange, and went to Harvard. I don't remember how it came up, but anyway, he and his wife, Petra, both went to Harvard. Everybody in this house is so smart and young and good-looking! There's also Frank, Bob's best friend, and his girlfriend, Sharon, who was Bob's old girlfriend, and Digger, who also went to Harvard, and whose girlfriend is coming up later this month. It's funny, but my first reaction was that these people are better than me, and that I don't deserve to be here. I mean, they all paid a lot of money for their shares in the house, and I'm here because I'm in Joanne's Debtors Anonymous group. So immediately, the first thing I did was volunteer to do everyone's laundry. And you know what? They said no. They told me to come out on the lawn and play touch football with them, which I did. After a couple of minutes, though, the ball hit me in the face, and even though everyone wanted me to continue playing, I was strong enough to know what I really wanted. Which was to stop playing touch football. So I volunteered to do the grocery shopping and I came out on the lawn and between plays we made a list. And I realized something. I had intended to pay for my food by, you know, paying one sixth or one seventh, depending, of the grocery bill. But these people wanted shrimp! I just can't afford to eat the way they eat. So I suggested that maybe I just buy my own food and eat separately, and they said that was silly, that they would kick in some for me. And I said okay, but only if I can do a little extra work, like cleaning the shrimp and cooking, and they said fine. So as I was making the dinner, I was thinking maybe I shouldn't be. Maybe I was being codependent, doing more than I had to do because I thought they're better than me. But then I remembered: I like to cook! And everybody loved it and we had a great dinner. Except Petra thought I could have used a little more garlic.

TODAY I WILL EAT A GREEN VEGETABLE AND A YELLOW VEGETABLE!

It's a good thing I'm here. This beautiful vegetable garden was getting overgrown with weeds. It's hard to believe that anyone would pour their love and care into such a beautiful garden and not be around when it bore fruit, or vegetable, or whatever, but evidently the owners of this place are in some financial difficulty and needed to rent the place out. Anyway, it's a good thing I like digging in the garden, because these things were in danger of getting choked off. And who can beat fresh vegetables from the garden? Look at this eggplant! It's beautiful! And these zucchini!? My Dad always had a garden, at least till I was about fourteen, when he just couldn't make the effort anymore. But when I was small he'd take me into the garden with him. It was kind of a special thing between me and him, because Donnie and Jodie just weren't interested. And he taught me a lot, like how to pinch off the excess tomato suckers. Like this one here . . . I'm sorry I'm getting upset . . . Okay . . . I'm Okay. I just haven't talked to my family since June. Anyway, this weeding is a lot of work. But it's worth it. My Mom would take this big zucchini here and stuff it with meat and cheese and this cream sauce till you could not locate the vegetable matter to save your life. Well, I'm cooking again tonight and we're having ratatouille! And I make a killer OA ratatouille! In fact, since I'm doing this book to help people, here's something concrete!

Stuart's Ratatouille

    1 eggplant (medium)
    2 zucchini (small)
    1 green pepper (medium)
    1 onion (medium)

4 tomatoes (medium)
1/8 cup olive oil
1 clove garlic

Cut the eggplant into 1/2-inch cubes. Slice up the zucchini. Chop the green pepper, onions, and tomatoes. Then throw everything into a pot, cover, and cook about fifteen or twenty minutes! That's it! Serves six people a low-cal healthy side dish! And here's a tip. Throw in some oregano and a hot red pepper for a zippy ratatouille Italiano!

Now don't tell me you didn't get anything out of this book!

I DID NOT DROP THE BOMB ON HIROSHIMA!

Last night around the dinner table, Digger mentioned that it was the anniversary of the atom bomb being dropped on Hiroshima. I think it came up because Sharon made a joke about Joanne's spirituality, and I kind of defended Joanne, even though, as you know, my Higher Power is very different from Joanne's. But since Joanne wasn't there to defend herself, I said something. Digger wondered how I could believe in a God who allowed Hiroshima to happen. I thought of Steve, who is Jewish and grew up with the Holocaust pounded into his head, and who has a real hard time turning his will over to a Higher Power. I made the point that those people who do these horrible things aren't in touch with their Higher Power and maybe that's why they do these horrible things. And Frank said that was stupid, because Harry Truman supposedly was religious and that some of the worst crimes in history have happened in the name of religion. Then Dirk defended Harry Truman, saying that he saved a lot of American lives by dropping the bomb, but Frank said Truman could have just dropped the bomb on Mt. Fuji, and the Japanese would have seen all the snow melt off the top of the mountain and have surrendered. Petra said she didn't think Harry Truman *was* religious, and then I said that twelve-step programs aren't religious, they're spiritual, and I explained the steps. And Frank scoffed at the third step, *"Make a decision to turn our will and our lives over to the care of God as we understood Him."* How could I turn my will over to a God who allowed the Holocaust and Hiroshima and child abuse and famine? And I said that *my* Higher Power didn't do those things, that my Higher Power was the part of me connected to the zucchini and the peppers and the onion and the eggplant and the tomatoes we were eating. And I was about to say that it was the part of me that felt connected to the people at the table, but Dirk cut me off and said something that made everyone laugh and then I didn't feel very connected to the people at the table. And then my head started to spin and I couldn't concentrate, but Frank said something about stupidity being the thing that really leads to the Holocaust and Hiroshima. And for a brief moment there I actually kind of felt somehow responsible for all the collective past horrors of mankind. Well, as someone once said in an Al-Anon meeting. "I didn't make the sun come up." And I don't make it go down.

I Don't Have to Like Everyone, and They Don't Have to Like Me!!

I called Carl, my OA sponsor, about my dinner conversation about Hiroshima. Carl said he thought I was most upset because I think these people don't like me. Then he said something he's said a thousand times before: "Stuart, if someone doesn't like you, it's their problem." Then I kicked myself for not thinking that at the time. And, of course, as soon as I wore that attitude into the kitchen, Digger came up to me and actually kind of apologized. He said that Dirk and Frank like to show how smart they are. Digger said Dirk thinks he's smarter because he went to Harvard, and Frank has a chip because he went to a state school, but he makes more money than Dirk. Then Petra came in and asked me if I wanted to go on a bike ride with the group. Well, I hope to get in shape up here, so I said yes. So we all went on these twelve-speeds and little did I know they were talking about a thirty-mile marathon! Digger stayed back with me as the others sped away out of sight. We got to talking, and it turns out that Digger is really, really wealthy. His great-great-great-grandfather literally built a railroad. In fact, if I told you his last name, you'd recognize which railroad. But Digger isn't really interested in the railroad and hasn't figured out what he wants to do. He says it's like he's been paralyzed by having so much money. He said he thought he was kind of pathetic, a thirty-four-year-old without a job. I said I was a forty-year-old without a job, and I think it made him feel better. Anyway, we decided to bike back home and go fishing, and there we were, sitting in the boat, two guys with our lines in the water, unemployed, but worth about thirty million between us!

I AM A CREATIVE PERSON!

It's funny how sometimes when you start to give someone else advice, you hear yourself suggesting things you could be doing yourself, but didn't think of or didn't give yourself permission to think. I told Digger that maybe he should look at having thirty million dollars as an opportunity to do something that normally is very low paying, like being a teacher or a poet. Digger told me he used to write short stories, but had given up. I told him to keep trying, that the worst he could do is write a bad short story and what's the harm in that? That's when I realized that *I've* always wanted to write short stories, but always have been afraid to because I thought they'd be bad. So, anyway, here's the name of the story I'm writing . . . "The Dysfunctional Forest." I haven't figured out what happens yet, but I have some of the names of the characters. Grandiose Bear, Rage-aholic Raccoon, and the Chipmunk brothers—Sad, Mad, Bad, Glad, and Had (because he feels like he's been had). I want it to be a book for the Inner Child. An Inner Children's book!

BOB AND JOANNE ARE BACK TOGETHER.

Wouldn't you know it! I had just started having the perfect time here, cooking, working in the garden, fishing with Digger, writing my short story (I've added Obese Otter, who gets stuck trying to get out of Sex-aholic Squirrel's tree home), and cleaning up for everyone. Now Bob and Joanne are back together, and I'm happy for them, but they've decided they want to use their share in the summer house after all. They're coming up today and after dinner (I'm making stuffed peppers!) Digger's driving me back to the city. It's actually a little sad. But you know what? It's a good sad!

DOGGONE IT, PEOPLE LIKE ME!

I don't have to leave after all! Last night at dinner everyone decided I could stay on a futon in the utility room. Petra was worried that I wouldn't have any privacy, but I offered to do everyone's laundry so they won't feel like they're trespassing on my territory. Then I told them the story about my Mom washing my address book and refused to take responsibility for what's in people's pockets, and everybody laughed, even Frank. So how do you like that!? These people like me!

I KNOW ME!

There is so much to do around here that if I'm not careful, I could easily get overwhelmed. There's the shopping, the laundry, the garden, the cooking, and yesterday I mowed a good part of the lawn. Digger says I shouldn't be doing all this stuff, but I told him I know me: if I didn't do this, I would feel so unentitled to stay here. After all, everybody's paying a share but me. But I have to remember to carve out some time for me. So after I clear the breakfast dishes I'm sitting down and working on "The Dysfunctional Forest." I've decided I like Grandiose Lion better than Grandiose Bear. I know lions are in jungles, not forests, but hey, this is my story, and if me and my inner child want a lion in our forest, that's okay!

IT'S A CUNNING, BAFFLING, POWERFUL DISEASE. III

I didn't get to work on "The Dysfunctional Forest" yesterday, because I spent a lot of time on the phone with Steve. He's really confused, and I don't think I helped him very much. He had a big fight with his wife at the marriage counselor's. Evidently during the session, he complained that she had never made a formal amends to him. I told Steve that I'm not sure there is such a thing as a *formal* amends and asked him if she had ever just said she was sorry for putting him through stuff because she was an alcoholic. He said that she made the exact same point, and he admitted that once or twice she had said she was sorry, but he felt that he was entitled to a more *detailed* amends. I said that it almost sounded like he was asking her to beg for forgiveness, and Steve said Dr. Best had said the same thing. But Steve said he got angry and he said something he kind of regrets. He told me he compared his wife to Hitler, and I said, "How exactly?" And he said that he told his wife that he realized alcoholism was a disease, but that Hitler had had a disease, too, paranoid schizophrenia, or something. Then he said he got up and was ranting around the doctor's office acting out asking Hitler for an amends, and then started detailing some of the stuff she did while she was drunk, and then he screamed at her, pretending she was Hitler and said, "What about the six million Jews?!" So things aren't too good with Steve. Me? Aside from feeling powerless to help Steve, I'm great. Everybody loves my cooking. I made a marinara sauce from the tomatoes in the garden and it was a big hit. But I got to get going. Digger's girlfriend is coming up from the city, so I want to wash his linens and run the vacuum around his room. I just have to be careful to put some time aside for myself. I don't want to get a resentment about doing all this housework!

TODAY I WILL MIND MY OWN BUSINESS!

Yesterday was one of the strangest days of my life, and I've had some pretty strange ones. I don't know where to start. Okay, first of all, I think Digger may have some kind of drug problem, which really upsets me. I went into his room to clean up, which I guess I shouldn't have done without asking him. I thought I was doing him a favor, but this just goes to show that I'm losing my sense of boundaries around here. Anyway, I was pulling the vacuum cleaner into his room and I backed into this table and I guess I must have knocked some drugs off the table, because . . . well, I vacuumed all this white powder off the rug and then I realized it had spilled off the table. Anyway, Digger came running in and he yelled at me, and it really hurt my feelings. I still freak out when I'm yelled at. Later in the garden he apologized for yelling, and I apologized for cleaning his room without asking, and I suggested maybe we go fishing, hoping he might want to talk about it, but he said he wanted to go to town to pick up some stuff for his girlfriend, who is the next big part of this story. So around dinnertime his girlfriend comes driving up. I'm in the kitchen cooking (eggplant parmigiana) and I look out at the driveway, and my God, I see this real familiar woman. And as Digger was carrying her bags into the house, I realized. It's Julia! Remember Julia, from the public relation's firm owned by Ted, the sex addict? Remember she was the queen bitch? Remember I said she kind of looks like a smaller, more Italian Julia Roberts? Remember that? Remember she worked on the PH&J thing with me? Remember how awful she was to me? Anyway, when I saw her I just wanted to bolt out of the house, away from this woman. And I decided then and there, between vacuuming up drugs and this woman being in the house, I was too uncomfortable to stay in this situation. So anyway, Digger leads her into the kitchen, and I am just praying that this woman doesn't remember me. And she looks up at me and gets this incredibly embarrassed look on her face and says, "Oh my, God. Stuart. Stuart, I am so sorry. I owe you an amends!" To make a long story short, we talked; Julia is in program (Al-Anon), and she is one terrific, courageous, wonderful girl. I just don't know whether to tell her about Digger and, you know . . . the drugs.

I AM NOT ALONE!

Julia and I found an Al-Anon meeting not too far from here. Julia's father was an alcoholic. At least the father she lived with. She's never met her real father, who was some Italian guy her mom had an affair with. Julia's father, the one she lived with, found out when she was about five, but it must have been pretty easy to tell Julia wasn't his, because all the other kids—there are five—are blond and blue-eyed. Julia's father really took it out on her and made her feel like she didn't belong. And I think that's Julia's main feeling in life—feeling like she doesn't belong. That's what's so great about Al-Anon meetings: you feel like you're not alone, that you *do* belong. And even though there were only about ten people at this little meeting, a woman shared about just the right thing. Obsessing. Because I had been obsessing all day about whether to tell Julia about vacuuming in Digger's room. Julia really likes Digger and says he's very different from all the other men she's chosen in her life, who were emotionally unavailable. She likes Digger because he's not a workaholic or high-powered achievement freak like her other men. Do I tell her? Is it my business? The woman at the Al-Anon meeting gave me the answer: if I stop obsessing, I'll know. Well, I've gotta go make breakfast.

TODAY I WILL WORK ON ME!

I've been paying so much attention to Julia and all the work I have up here that I haven't been able to really pay any attention to Steve. When I finally returned his call yesterday, his wife answered and told me he was at the downtown Marriott. When I reached Steve, he told me that Dr. Best had suggested he move out for a while, that he and his wife could use a break from each other and each work on themselves. And I think that might be wise. It really is impossible to be happy in a relationship until we know and love and respect ourselves. I think that's why I haven't even thought about dating. I'm still working on me. And believe me, Steve can use some work on himself! While he was talking, I realized something. Steve hadn't said anything funny to me in the last two weeks, which is unlike him, and I think a real sign that he's at a bad point in his recovery. Anyway, he wants to fly Donna in from Philadelphia, you remember, the nurse he met at the shame conference. Dr. Best strongly advised against it, saying "You're working on your marriage now." I didn't want to give advice, but when Steve asked me what I thought he should do, I said, "Maybe Dr. Best is right. Maybe this is not a good time to bury yourself in Donna." And then Steve said that's exactly what he wants to do, bury himself in Donna, which is at least a little funny, and made me feel like maybe I was helping a little. And speaking of helping, Steve is moving into my apartment. It works out well for both of us. Steve'll pay my August rent, and believe me it's cheaper than the downtown Marriott!

I COULD HAVE ROZ WEINMAN FIRED!

Joanne says this is definitely H.P., for which she was
roundly ridiculed by Frank and Dirk. But get this—Julia
represents Tantamount Cable, a.k.a. Roz Weinman's employer.
See, after joining Al-Anon, Julia left Ted's public relations firm,
because she realized Ted was a dysfunctional sex addict. Julia
then started her own firm, which I think took tremendous courage, and shows you what recovery can do. Anyway, she's doing
very well, and her big client is Tantamount Cable, which is
owned and run by this guy, Pete Tartaglione, who is, get this, a
recovering mobster! Literally. A mobster in recovery. No, he
doesn't go to MA. (That's a joke. There is no MA. Well, actually
there is: Marijuana Anonymous. So Mobsters Anonymous would
have to be MoA. Unless there's a Morphine Anonymous . . .)
Anyway. The point is, Tartaglione goes to ACOA. Evidently,
this guy's father was a big Chicago mobster and a bigger alcoholic. Pete inherited the business and was supposedly a real big
crook. That's how he got the cable company. Anyway, he fell in
love with this Irish girl, whose father was also an alcoholic, and
Pete's family went nuts on him when he married her. Then his
dad was garroted. And Pete's family went to war with another
family. That's when his wife realized her life was unmanageable
and started going to ACOA meetings, and pretty soon Pete
started going too. Now all his business is legit, although he says
it's now actually harder to maintain rigorous honesty in his business dealings than it used to be. Anyway, Julia says she could
talk to Pete and Roz Weinman would be toast. I mean fired, not
rubbed out. Joanne says it's H.P., but I don't think H.P. would
give me this kind of power over someone else. So I slept on it,
and I think I know what I want to do. I want Julia to ask Pete to
ask Roz nicely to put me back on the air, and if she refuses, then
he should insist on it. Then if she refuses again, he should rec-

ommend that she go to OA. Then if she refuses again, he should *insist* that she go to OA. Then if she refuses again, he should tell her if she doesn't go, he'll fire her. Then if she refuses, well, then I think she doesn't really want the job.

I HAVE MY SHOW BACK!!!

I am so scared! I got the show back! Roz Weinman told Pete Tartaglione that she loves my show and that there must have been some misunderstanding between us. Yeah, right. So *Daily Affirmations with Stuart Smalley* is back on public access cable in a week! All this happened and I didn't have to move an inch from this country house. It all just came to me! Whether or not that's Higher Power, I have been praying that I will have the wisdom, courage, and creativity to do better shows than my last batch, which were not very good. But that's okay. I am so terrified! But that's okay. I just have to own the terror. Oh boy, what should I do my first show on? How about the feeling I have right now? That when anything good happens to me, I immediately freak out? This is a good topic! It's because I think I don't deserve good things to happen. And I'm always waiting for the next shoe to drop. Okay, this is good. Okay, that's my first show. Okay. How I freak out when anything positive happens. I don't know, maybe that's not so good. No, it's good.

I CAN BREAK OLD PATTERNS!!

O kay. I'm starting to feel myself getting overwhelmed. Which is good. At least I can detect it right away, before it gets out of hand. That just shows you how far I've come. I just have to remember, first things first. First I write my affirmation, which I'm doing now. Then I clean up after last night. Then I make breakfast. Then I wash the dishes. Then I water the garden. No, maybe I should water the garden after I do this. It's going to be hot today, and my Dad always taught me to water early so the sun doesn't burn it off. Otherwise you're wasting water. Anyway, I have all this stuff to do. I should make a list. But see, that falls into my pattern. Just before I get totally overwhelmed, I start making lists. Then I usually lose the lists. Okay, first thing is to recognize what I'm freaked out about, which is the fact that I got my show back. Maybe if it hadn't been so sudden I wouldn't be so scared. So this is really about the show and not about all the chores I have to do, except it is because I'm afraid I won't have enough time to really sit down and think about the show, which starts in five days. I have five days to figure out what I'm doing, and I really haven't even had time to work on "The Dysfunctional Forest," except that I thought of a new character, Paralyzed Porcupine, who has writer's block. Julia says I shouldn't be doing all this work around here, and she helps when she can, but Digger kind of wants her to be with him a lot. In fact, I think something's going on between them now. She says she likes him because he's not a workaholic, but I think somewhere in there she's attracted to Digger because he's from this wealthy family and went to Harvard. Not because Julia cares about money, but because she grew up in the projects and went to a junior college, and she thinks Digger is a step up somehow. Maybe I can do a show on this. It would be about, let's see . . . Oh God, I have no idea, I'm completely blank. I am so scared!

I CAN SLIP WITHOUT FALLING!

I just lost it today. I screamed at Frank. At lunch he put a cigarette out in a glob of peanut butter, which is incredibly obnoxious to wash off, and I just lost it. In fact, I called him an inconsiderate asshole, which he is, but I think when you lose your temper, it only hurts you. Julia said the whole thing was an Al-Anon slip, which of course it was. But that's okay. Someone in an Al-Anon meeting once said it's okay to slip, the problem is when you use one slip to trigger another slip and you're slipping and sliding and falling all over the place. It's like that thing I keep hearing comedians say. "Help! I've fallen and I can't get up!" I don't know where it's from, but I keep hearing comedians say it on TV, and people laugh. So I tried to trace the reason I slipped, and of course, it's the show. So I just decided it was time to really sit down and think about the show. So I got out there on the sitdown mower and just mowed for a good three hours. No distractions. I just zoned out and mowed. It was heaven! And I thought of a couple topics for my TV show and realized what I had totally left out of The Dysfunctional Forest. Birds.

I AM WHO I AM WHEREVER I AM!

I've been faxing Andrea the pages and periodically she's been telling me to either go back to the city or stop doing so much of the house and yard work up here. She called yesterday after she read I had my show back and begged me to go back to the city. She said I needed to focus on my show. And she's right. It's just that Steve is living in my place now, and I think it would be unfair to ask him to move out, and there's really only room for one person. I'd have to sleep on my couch or the floor, which come to think of it is where I'm sleeping now, although the futon is pretty comfortable. The point is I can focus up here if I really want to, like on the mower. Sometimes we try to escape from our problems by going somewhere else, even though in this case I would be going home. But I am grateful for Andrea's and Carl's concern. (He called too.) Starting tomorrow, I am scaling back on my household chores. I'll just tell the others that I'd be willing to pay, you know, on a pro rata basis, for my share of the house or personally pay for a housekeeper with the rent money I'm getting from Steve. Anyway, all that starts tomorrow. Today I have to get the house ready for this big party. Frank and Bob and Dirk have invited some of their commodity broker friends for a big blowout, and I've got a lot of cooking to do!

I AM IN JAIL!

For some reason they let me keep this little tape recorder, and not my belt. I guess you can't hang yourself with a tape recorder. It turns out that Digger is not worth thirty million dollars. He's a drug dealer. He did go to Harvard though, but his great-great-great-grandfather didn't start a railroad. His great-great-great-grandfather's brother did. I haven't seen Julia since they arrested us, but Digger is here in this cell along with Frank and Dirk and a lot of their friends from the commodities exchange. That's why I'm talking so low. Anyway, Digger seems surprisingly calm, although everyone else is pretty agitated. Frank has been screaming at the policeman all night about how bad this will be for the summer house industry up here. I feel so humiliated. Arrested for cocaine possession. Did you know that I have never even taken a drink of alcohol? Not one. I'm afraid I'll turn out like Dad or Donnie. I should have said something. I should have told Julia about vacuuming in Digger's room. This could have been avoided. I should have moved out like Andrea said. Okay . . . calm down. This is not my fault. This is not my fault. God grant me the serenity to accept the things I cannot . . . *You* shut up! . . . No, Frank, *you* shuttup! . . .

TODAY I WILL LOOK AT THE POSITIVE SIDE OF ANY HORRIBLE THING THAT HAPPENS!

Maybe getting arrested was not such a bad thing. The trauma made me forget how nervous I was about my show. I'm back in my apartment in the city now. I've gotten so used to sleeping on a futon that I've decided that, for the rest of the month at least, Steve and I can share the apartment. And later today I can go down to the studio and check out my set. It's really just what they call a twofold (a flat that folds in two) and a mirror. I'm lucky, because, unbeknownst to Roz Weinman, they've been keeping the stuff in storage. I'm sure she would have had it destroyed had she thought about it. Oh. Yesterday we were arraigned and in about a month there's some kind of trial or hearing. Julia, of course, was very upset, but probably more angry, at Digger. On his lawyer's advice, Digger didn't admit that he's a drug dealer, and that Julia and I were innocent bystanders, at least not to the police. He did apologize to Julia, and said that he'd still like to see her. She said she wasn't interested in seeing a drug addict, and Digger explained that he doesn't actually use drugs, that he's just a dealer, that drug dealers who use drugs get in a lot of trouble. Anyway, Julia says the whole thing has brought up a lot of issues with her. The biggest one being her relationships with men. She's known Digger for two months, which she says makes it her second longest relationship ever, and can't believe how blind she was to who he is. I made an amends for not telling her about how I vacuumed up the drugs in his room, and Julia kind of yelled at me for not telling her, but then she made an immediate amends. She said from now on I could tell her anything about anything and it would be okay. So I told her that maybe this was what she really needed to force her to look at her relationships with men. Maybe this was the best thing that ever happened to her. Julia yelled at me, and about two minutes later made an immediate amends. I really like her.

I'VE LOST MY SHOW.

'll make this short, because I just want to go buy some ice cream, then get in bed. The police blotter in the local Wisconsin newspaper listed me as being arrested for cocaine possession. Somehow Roz Weinman got ahold of it, and . . . I don't want to go into it . . . I—I don't blame her.

You Know What? Chicken Butt!

I didn't get it either. But when Brent asked, "You know what?" over the phone, and I said "What?" he said, "Chicken butt." I asked him what it meant, and he said, "Guess what it means." And I said, "What?" And he said, "Chicken butt." That's when I got it. He was being silly. You see, "butt" rhymes with "what." You know what? Chicken butt! So I immediately got out of bed and got dressed to go down to Brent's uncle's Ford dealership to answer phones for the Muscular Dystrophy telethon. It was the first time I'd been out of bed except to get ice cream (Borden's chocolate) since Julia called me to say that she had lost the Pete Tartaglione account. She said Pete had said that he was sorry, but that he used to be involved with drugs himself (the distribution of), and he didn't need the bad press. So I've spent the last two weeks feeling sorry for myself, on the pity pot as they say, despite all the best efforts of everyone. Steve had to move out; he couldn't stand it. Andrea flew in, and she and Carl did the usual. But I wouldn't budge. Finally, she called Brent down in Florida. I guess Andrea thought it would be impossible for me feel sorry for myself if a kid in a wheelchair called. But I just thought it was a cheap trick, so when I got on the phone with Brent, I think I was kind of resentful toward him for being in a wheelchair. Wow. I can't believe I said that. I guess I thought, "At least he has an excuse." And then he said, "You know what?" And I guess the whole chicken butt thing made me realize Brent doesn't think about having an excuse or not having an excuse. And instead of feeling more sorry for him than I felt for me, I kind of felt . . . just stupid. So Brent told me to go out to his uncle's dealership in Elgin and answer phones. Which I did. And it was fun! Much more fun than lying in bed eating ice cream.

TODAY I WILL ACCEPT THE GOOD THAT CAME OUT OF THE BAD!

Andrea and Carl are engaged! They announced it yesterday at lunch before Andrea had to fly back to New York for an important meeting at Dell. She looked radiant, and I'd say about a hundred and forty pounds lighter than when I first saw her walk through my door to rescue me from one of my funks. We all laughed at how if it wasn't for my severe shame spirals, Andrea and Carl would never have met. Carl joked that every horrible thing that ever happened to me has really worked to his advantage. And we started talking about Higher Power and what's predestined and that stuff, and I got a little confused. But I realized something. I always used to think that Acceptance was about accepting the bad things we cannot change. Sometimes we have to remember to accept or let in the good things that happen, and yes, the good things that happen as a result of the horrible things we cannot change. God, I love this Program!

I'M GOOD ENOUGH, I'M SMART ENOUGH, AND DOGGONE IT, PEOPLE LIKE ME! II

I keep saying this over and over today, because I really need to. Steve and I went out for coffee last night, after the Al-Anon meeting. He shared during the meeting, and he's been having a hard time, living at a Holiday Inn, missing his kids, pining for Donna, yet trying to work on his marriage. I thought that maybe I could cheer him up a little at coffee, so I told him about yesterday's affirmation about how you can accept the good that's come out of the bad, and then joked how he never would have met me if it hadn't been for his wife's drinking. That's when Steve looked really bad, and then he said he had something to tell me. I guess he had been agonizing about it for a couple weeks. He told me he didn't want me to be his sponsor anymore, that he was thinking of asking David from our Monday noon meeting. I realized immediately what this was about. How many of us would like to see their sponsor lying in bed, wallowing in self-pity, spooning ice cream into his fat face? Well, that's what Steve witnessed for three days, seventy-two straight hours of wallowing, before he moved out. Steve felt horrible telling me, but at least he was direct and honest. He said he loved me, and I believed him, but I guess I also really don't believe that anyone can love such a pathetic fool. Which is why I keep saying I'm good enough, I'm smart enough, and doggone it, people like me. I'm good enough, I'm smart enough, and doggone it, people like me. I'm good enough, I'm . . . Oh God, who am I kidding?

THIS TIME I WAS IN BED FOR ONLY FIVE DAYS!

Which is progress! Of course, it came right on the heels of a longer one, but that's okay. The point is I think I'm getting more resilient. Usually when I take to my bed, my friends need at least six or seven tries before they can get me to budge. But this time Carl and Steve did it in one visit! Steve suspected something was wrong when he kept getting a busy signal and he called Carl and they both came over. I answered the door in my pajamas and crawled back to my bed and my Toll House cookies. I thought Steve was going to lie and say he wanted me back as a sponsor. But he didn't. Instead Carl told me something he had never told me before. He told me that he had been fired as a sponsor once, too, although he didn't use that word, fired. I couldn't believe it. I mean, Carl is the wisest, most wonderful sponsor in the whole world. I would weigh four hundred pounds if it weren't for Carl. Then, I thought, "Oh, it must have been some nut who fired Carl." But no, Carl told me the sponsee was Ernie, Carl's best friend. Steve jumped in and said that just because he had a new sponsor, it didn't mean he didn't want me as a friend. Then he asked me a very profound favor. He wanted to do his fifth step with me. The fifth step is "Admitted to God, to ourselves, and to another human being the exact nature of our wrongs." He wanted me to be the human being. Steve said he liked his new sponsor, but he was too afraid to do his fifth step with him. He said that for all my faults, I was the most open and accepting person he had ever met, and that I was the only human being he felt he could admit his wrongs to. I was moved to tears and put down the bag of cookies and hugged Steve.

TODAY I WILL MAKE A SEARCHING AND FEARLESS MORAL INVENTORY OF MYSELF!

If I want to! I told Steve I was ready to hear his fifth step anytime, but he told me he hadn't quite finished his fourth step yet, which is "Made a searching and fearless moral inventory of ourselves." The fifth step, basically, is to tell your fourth step to God, yourself, and someone else. I did my fourth step about three years ago, and I have to tell you, it changed my life. That's right, changed my life. I know what you're thinking, but believe me, I used to be a lot worse than this. So far, this has been the best year of my life. Without question! So you can imagine! Anyway, I did my fourth step about a hundred and ten pounds ago, and I have to tell you, it was like a hundred-and-ten-pound load off my shoulders. Sure it was scary. But when it was done, what a relief! And not just because I had finished some painful task. But because I realized that I wasn't really such a horrible person and because I knew more about myself and what I was really about. And that's kind of exciting! It was also exciting to realize what simple honesty and humility could achieve. It was also exciting to think I could actually get rid of these faults and be a better, happier person. It was exciting! And when Steve told me he was working on his fourth step, I was excited for *him*. And then I remembered that the fourth step is really an ongoing process, something I can do every day until I am totally flaw-less, which at this rate will be sometime in the year 3000! So this is exciting! I'm going to do *my* fourth step!

I AM NOT AN EXHIBITIONIST!

I've been working on my fourth step for a day now, and I had been toying with the idea of just printing it on these pages, you know, like my ratatouille recipe. But I've decided that, even though you know most of my deep, dark secrets, that might be a little unseemly. In fact, that maybe is one of my faults, which is that I can go on about my faults to people I hardly even know. Though I feel I know you, dear reader. Even though I obviously don't. Anyway, you probably know my faults better than me. So just for fun, here's a multiple-choice test. Which one of these defects of character is in my fourth step?

A. GRANDIOSITY
B. SELF-PITY
C. FEARFULNESS
D. ANGER
E. WILLFULNESS
F. GLUTTONY
G. OBVIOUS WRITING
H. ALL OF THE ABOVE!

I REFUSE TO FEEL GUILTY!

I don't know if feeling guilty is a moral defect, but it sure doesn't do me a lot of good. When I feel guilty, it's really hard for me to get anything done. And then usually I feel guilty about that. Then I wallow in the guilt. I think wallowing itself is a big issue with me. Because sometimes after I wallow, I feel guilty about wallowing. Remember a few months ago I wrote about having feelings about your feelings? This is like having defects about your defects. Anyway, I think that sometimes feeling guilty is okay and is a sign of health, and sometimes it's a sign that we feel too responsible for everything and forget that we don't control the world. So I guess sometimes guilt is just an extension of my grandiosity. But I'm not sure what to do with the guilt I feel today. Because *it's my Mom's birthday! And I don't want to call her.* And I mean, why should I? The last time I spoke to Mom she was going along with the rest of my family, who were threatening to sue me if I publish this book, and I guess still are. The odd part is that she probably doesn't realize I'm angry with her. Which is even more infuriating. I could call her and be honest and say "Happy birthday, Mom, I love you, but you know I'm really angry with you." And she'd say, "Really, why?" And I'd say, "Don't you remember Donnie and Dad telling me the family will sue me if I publish the book?" And Mom would say something like, "Oh, honey, are you still upset (not angry, which is the word I used, but upset) about that?" And I'd say, "Well, Mom, what does that mean? Does it mean that it's okay for me to publish the book?" And Mom would say, "Well, you wrote some pretty horrible things about Dad and Donnie and Jodie." (Not her, you notice, did you notice that?) And I'd say, "Yeah, Mom, but they were all true." And she'd say, "Now, Stuart, you know how you've always exaggerated things, especially since you joined that ACLU group." And I'd say, "ACOA,

Mom, I've told you a million times, Adult Children of Alcoholics." And she'd say, "Well, I have a hard time remembering it, because I don't understand why you would be in a group by that name." And by then, I'd be screaming. Okay. I'm sending a mailgram.

TODAY I WILL NOT PROCRASTINATE!

Julia and I went to coffee after last night's ACOA meeting. I told her I was doing my fourth step and that I had written a lot about procrastination. Julia doesn't procrastinate; she just goes out and does things. After she lost Tartaglione's cable TV account she went right out and got Lifeline Cable, which . . . Oh, by the way, all the cocaine charges against me and Julia were dropped. Digger plea-bargained, pled guilty, told the truth about us, and I think informed on whoever it was he bought his cocaine from. So he's out of jail, and he called Julia to apologize. She said she didn't scream at him, which is real progress for her, but she told him she never wanted to see him again, which I would have thought was obvious. But you know what? Julia says that in spite of everything, part of her wanted to see him again. But that's the old part, the part that goes for dangerous, addictive, unavailable men. That would be in Julia's fourth step: "I am attracted to dangerous, addictive, unavailable men." Which brings me back to procrastination. Julia is now becoming a cheerleader for my show, and she wants me to try to get it on this Lifeline channel. But this isn't public access; this is the real thing. I'd get paid! That is so scary! Anyway, I need to put an audition tape together. I don't know where to begin actually. Believe it or not, I never taped my show. I was too afraid to watch it. I think they may have some tape of me down at the studio. Of course, I'd have to talk to Roz Weinman. So I guess that's what I have to do. Talk to Roz Weinman. I can do that tomorrow.

FIRST THINGS FIRST!

I was going to call Roz Weinman today, but Steve is going to come over and we're going to do his fifth step. And I really owe him my full attention.

I DON'T HAVE TO BEAT MYSELF UP!

Listening to Steve's fourth step, the first thing I started to do was to compare myself. Which is sick. But I couldn't help it. Steve's fourth step was so . . . complete. Of course, a lot of it I had heard before. But a lot of it I hadn't. For instance, Steve thinks he's a sex addict, which I don't think he is. He says he's masturbating almost every day now, but I'm not quite sure how that is a moral defect; Freud once said, and believe me, I am not a big fan of Freud (talk about grandiosity!), but Freud once said that the only thing to be ashamed of about masturbating is not doing it well. That evidently isn't Steve's problem. I think he's just racked with guilt. Steve believes that his problems in life come from his obsessive need for orgasms. Steve says that's why he got married. His wife was his high school sweetheart and they got married right out of college—Steve thinks simply because he wanted to have sex regularly. I think he thinks this because he hates her so much right now that he's forgotten why or even that he loved her. Then Steve hit me with the big bombshell. Donna wasn't the first extramarital affair he had had. Which was news to me. As Steve read this part of his fourth step (off his laptop computer) he started to shake. Steve said that a couple times on business trips he had slept with other women. He said he felt that somehow his wife had sensed this and that that's what made her drink. He said he knows that's not true, but he can't help feeling it. Then he just started crying. No one I know is smarter than Steve, and I know that he's read all the literature and been in Al-Anon over a year and heard the three *C*'s (I didn't *Cause* it, I can't *Cure* it, and I can't *Control* it) a million times. But somewhere, deep down, Steve still feels responsible for his wife's drinking. But what Steve is killing himself over is the kids. Steve said he never had an affair here in town because he couldn't stand the idea of taking even five minutes (some affair!)

away from his kids for something like that. And now, Steve only sees his kids on weekends, and it's eating him up. After we were done, Steve looked totally drained. I told Steve that he had done a pretty good job of using his fourth step to beat himself up. I told him I thought he thinks he's a sex addict because, aside from two nights with Donna in Baltimore, he's been celibate for about seven or eight months. That would make almost anyone obsess about sex to the point of thinking they're an addict. I told him he had done a great job of constructing a "case" against himself, which is the way Steve thinks. Steve said he knew all this. But that maybe he had needed to write it down and tell it to someone before he could tell whether it was true or not. We had tea, and Steve started to lighten up. I think he was relieved. And I think it was because he realized in his gut that most of what he had written wasn't really true.

GOD GRANT ME COURAGE!

Roz Weinman's assistant says she has five of my shows on tape. One of the shows was my "You're Only as Sick as Your Secrets" show, which was one of my very best. I'm sure if I showed it to the people at Lifeline they might possibly consider giving me a chance to maybe do a pilot or something. I'm so scared. Anyway, Roz's assistant isn't sure Roz will release the tapes to me, and today I am going to talk to Roz and make an amends for calling her a horrible, nasty, dysfunctional bitch. I'm kind of torn about that, because I think it destroys the whole purpose of amends if you're making them to get something from someone. But on the other hand, I don't know how realistic it would be to make this request without first apologizing. Maybe if I separate the amends and the request for the tape into two totally separate, distinct actions . . . First I'll make my amends, from the heart, totally letting go of the result. And then I will make the request in a forthright manner, standing up for myself, because I am worth standing up for. Okay, that's how I'm going to do it! Okay.

I STOLE THE TAPE!

I didn't sleep last night. I kept watching my show entitled, "This Is a Program of Rigorous Honesty!" over and over. It was on the tape, the tape I stole. Or rather a copy of the tape I stole. See, Roz Weinman kept me waiting outside her office for a couple hours again. Her assistant, Lori Jo, had the tape on her desk. Lori Jo told me that Roz was going to charge me four hundred dollars for the tape, supposedly to pay for dubbing or tape stock or something, but I knew Roz was just trying to make it difficult for me. So, after about an hour sitting outside Roz's office, Lori Jo went to lunch. I don't know exactly why, but suddenly my heart was pounding and I jumped up and grabbed the tape and ran into the elevator. By the time I hit the street I was sweating profusely. I grabbed a cab and raced over to Julia's office. She was in a meeting, but she came right out, and I told her what I had done. She told me I absolutely had to return the tape. Only not until I copied it! Julia gave it to her assistant, who made a copy right away, then gave me the original, and I raced back to Roz's office, beating Lori Jo by about two minutes. When Roz finally called me in about a half hour later, I made my amends—for calling her a horrible, nasty, dysfunctional bitch, not for stealing the tape. Roz did offer to sell me the tape for four hundred dollars, and when I said no, she started yelling at me. I think I was so upset about stealing the tape that I forgot myself and called her a "fat, disgusting c-nt," which I can't believe I said. It's probably the single ugliest word in the English language, and I don't mean "fat" or "disgusting." Anyway, I ran out of the room and into the elevator and cried all the way down. How did I ever get this desperate? This fearful? This out of control? I definitely have to fourth-step this stuff. I'm a mess.

And the worst thing is I still owe Roz Weinman an amends—for calling her a you-know-what, and for stealing her tape. And I guess in addition to an amends, I owe her four hundred dollars. Oh, God. I think I'll just try to get some sleep.

I HAVE FRIENDS!

Julia called Carl, and Carl called Steve. And they all came over. Andrea even called from New York. It's gotten to the point where if I want to take to my bed, I better rent a room somewhere without telling anyone. Steve thought it was ridiculous for me to feel I owe Roz four hundred dollars. Julia said the tape was rightfully mine in the first place, and that if anyone owed anyone an amends, Roz was the one who should do the apologizing. Carl says he doesn't want to give me advice, because he's my sponsor, but he suggested I meditate on this. Clear my mind of all my junk and ask my Higher Power who really owes whom what. So I did that. And my Higher Power came back with an answer. Screw Roz Weinman!

TODAY I WILL PUT IT OUT THERE!

Julia is editing my tape. She especially likes my show entitled "Today I Give Myself Permission to Succeed," which, in a sense, is what all this is about. After she's done editing, she'll give it to the head of programming at Lifeline. I know he'll hate it, but that's okay. At least I'm putting it out there. And sometimes you just got to put it out there. Because sometimes we're afraid to put ourselves out there, because we fear the rejection. Well, as Julia says, the rejection is short-term. It happens now and then it's over. But putting it out there is a way of life. If I put it out there one day at a time, the rewards are tremendous! So I'm putting it out there! Speaking of which, I'm still working on "The Dysfunctional Forest," and when I'm done, I'm going to send it to Andrea, you know, to put it out there. But in the meantime I started another story, "The Penguin That Could Fly." It's kind of autobiographical.

I'VE BEEN SUBPOENAED!

No, not for stealing Roz Weinman's tape. My family is suing Mr. Egeberg to compel him to grant an easement to the estate at the original three thousand dollars. I called Jodie, and she seemed kind of nervous and embarrassed on the phone and said she'd explain everything when I get home to Minneapolis tomorrow. So I'm not sure of all the details, but I think I have to give a deposition and maybe testify in court. And, again, I'm not certain of what the whole situation is, but I am pretty sure of one thing. Which is that my family wants me to lie.

WHEN I GO HOME TO VISIT MY FAMILY I WILL STAY IN A MOTEL!

think this is one of my best affirmations. In fact, I think this affirmation alone should win me the National Book Award. Not to be grandiose . . . It's just that I know this affirmation will actually save lives. Because if I was staying at home I would kill somebody or myself. I always knew my family was crazy, but they have reached new levels of insanity. Normally, they just deny things that are right in front of their noses. But now they're actually inventing realities that don't exist. For instance, Donnie's lawyer, who now represents the family—which is a book in itself, believe me—Donnie's lawyer drafted a *backdated* letter of acceptance of Mr. Egeberg's original three thousand dollars for the easement, which Jodie then signed. Now, that's not crazy, it's just dishonest. The crazy thing is that they now act like they believe Jodie really wrote and signed that letter back in May! We had a family meeting last night in the living room. Mom made beans and buns, and Jodie was stuffing her face and crying about paying for Kyle's swimming and how it's unfair for Kyle to have to live in a little apartment and how Kyle is the only one in the family who has a chance and how Mr. Egeberg is evil. Dad was drunk out of his mind and useless, and Donnie was stoned and couldn't even keep the sequence of events in his head. In a way, Mom was the only one who was really sober, which made talking to her the most frustrating, because all she could say was how crazy Mr. Egeberg is. (He's now asking $20,000 for a two-foot easement, which is kind of crazy, but he's obviously just pissed off.) But Mom just wouldn't see what was going on. It's like the elephant in the living room, which is this analogy for the denial that goes on in a family with an alcoholic. The only thing, I couldn't tell anymore who was an elephant and who was ignoring the elephant. As far as I'm concerned, I was watching four elephants lurch around my living room, and then one of the elephants, I think it was Donnie, said something about their "deal" with me. What deal? I said. Then Jodie explained. If I just deny that I ever had that conversation with Mr. Egeberg, the one where I told him we hadn't agreed to his three-thousand-dollar offer, if I just deny that, then the elephants will let me publish this book.

TODAY I WILL DO
WHAT I DO FOR THE RIGHT REASON!

Later today, I give my deposition. Donnie's lawyer says that if I lie it would be just my word against Mr. Egeberg's and we'd probably win, since there's nothing in writing refusing Mr. Egeberg's original offer. So if I lie, Jodie could probably move into Aunt Paula's house next month and Mom and Dad and Donnie could get their share of the inheritance. (What's left of it after the lawyer's bills.) I suppose I'd get some money too. And I could continue on writing my book, knowing it was okay with my family if I published it. I'm beginning to think it would be okay with Dad for me to write a three-paragraph description of him puking if there were five hundred dollars in it for him. I'm sorry. That's not true, it's just my anger. He'd probably do it for two-fifty. According to Steve, Hitler once said that every man has his price, but what's surprising is how low that price is. Okay. This is getting very negative. This has to be the first recovery book ever to use a kernel of wisdom from Adolf Hitler. I think my anger is just a cover. For my sadness. For my sense of betrayal. Do they really think I'd lie so I could publish this book? Besides, I can do it anyway, according to Andrea and the lawyer from Dell. This is just emotional blackmail. Well, I prayed to the Higher Power last night. Not to tell me what to do —I know what I'm going to do, I'm going to tell the truth—but to help me get through this. And H.P. answered. H.P. said, remember why you're telling the truth. You're going to tell the truth not because you're angry or sad or hurt, but because it's the right thing to do. So I will tell the truth and feel good about it!

MR. EGEBERG HAD A HEART ATTACK!

I didn't give my deposition yesterday. I got a call from Donnie's lawyer telling me the news about Mr. Egeberg. The poor man's in critical condition. Donnie said he hopes he dies, and I think Dad does, too, but Jodie's a little freaked out because she thinks that the lawsuit might have caused the heart attack. Gee, which one's the codependent? The odd thing is that in a way I felt a big sense of relief. Even though I had decided I was going to feel okay about going against my family, I guess I was fooling myself. I guess you can't control your feelings. Anyway, things are kind of on hold. We're waiting to see what happens to Mr. Egeberg. I've been praying for him and his family. When I first prayed, I prayed that he would recover and then be open to listening to me explain everything that's happened and then he would be more reasonable and just ask for something like five thousand dollars for the easement. I realized, of course, that I was praying for control over the situation, which is just not a healthy thing to be praying for. So then I prayed again for guidance, and Carl called and suggested that I consider getting out of here as soon as possible. So today I'm going to watch Kyle in a swim meet, and then I take the first bus back to Chicago. I've got to get back to my life!

TODAY I WILL DETACH WITH LOVE! II

Kyle won the swim meet. In fact, he set a record for eight-year-olds! I sat in these bleachers with Mom and Dad and Donnie and Jodie, and things were kind of awkward to say the least, because I had told Mom the other day how I was going to testify in my deposition, and I guess she told them. So everyone was kind of quiet. Until Kyle's race. He got out in the lead right away, and I couldn't believe it, but Dad started screaming, before even Jodie, then Mom joined in and me and Donnie, and we were all screaming for Kyle. By the time he hit the far end of the pool, Dad was jumping up and down, and Kyle came out of the turn way ahead of everybody else, and Donnie starts chanting, "Smalley . . . Smalley . . . Smalley!" which is now legally Kyle's last name. (He's been Kyle Skoag, Kyle Smalley, Kyle La Pierre, and now he's Kyle Smalley again.) Anyway, Kyle won by about ten feet and suddenly everybody was hugging everybody and jumping up and down. And a thought hit me, which was "This is how it used to be." Only, this isn't how it used to be. In fact, I can't remember us doing anything remotely like this. But I guess this is how I used to wish it would be. But then I thought that, at least for this moment, this was pretty good. Even if it did take an eight-year-old setting a meet record. Afterwards we all took Kyle out for ice cream at Bridgemans and Dad had a malted and even seemed happy about it. And despite one or two moments of ugliness (Dad started talking about how the rich Edina kids ate Kyle's dust), we all had a great time. And I realized I haven't been detaching with love. I've been detaching with hurt, detaching with scorn, detaching with anger, detaching with judgment. So I've decided to stay another day or two, so that I can detach properly.

TODAY I WILL ZIP THE LIP!

The motel was getting a little expensive, so I decided to stay with Jodie and Kyle. I had planned to sleep on the couch, but I forgot that that's where Kyle sleeps. So Jodie has this air mattress, and she and I tried to blow it up, and we were taking forever, so Kyle blew it up for us in about ten seconds. The kid's in shape! No wonder, he swims two hours every night at this swim club. I drove Kyle to practice, and on the way, Kyle seemed a little serious. So I tried something. I said, "You really got Grandpa excited last night. And you know what?" And Kyle said, "What?" And I said, "Chicken butt!" And Kyle just stared at me like I was crazy. So I tried it a few more times, and then explained it and how Brent taught it to me, and Kyle said he thought it was stupid. The fact is, Kyle thought that pretty much everything I said was stupid, so after a while I just shut my face. At practice Kyle was clearly the best swimmer, but I have to say I don't think he was enjoying it one bit. So later in the car I told Kyle that maybe he was taking the swimming a little too seriously, that winning isn't as important as enjoying the swimming. And he just looked at me like I was this humongous idiot. So I zipped the lip and just drove us home.

TODAY I WILL REMEMBER THAT ALCOHOLISM IS A FAMILY DISEASE!

Mr. Egeberg's spirit left his body yesterday. We got the call from Donnie's lawyer just as Kyle, me, and Jodie sat down to our macaroni and cheese dinner. (Kraft's Crap we used to call it growing up, but actually I kind of like it.) Jodie immediately started crying. She thinks we, the Smalley family, killed him. I told her Mr. Egeberg had to be in his eighties, and even if we did kill him, he probably lost five or ten years at most. It was my attempt at a joke, but Jodie was too far gone. She said that she let Donnie sue Mr. Egeberg because she was desperate. Then she told me that she hasn't even had enough money to pay for Kyle's swim club, that his coach is willing to let him swim for free as long as he keeps winning. She told me this with Kyle standing right there, which I couldn't believe, but I looked at Kyle and I realized he already knew. So I asked Kyle to go work on his homework in his mom's room, but Kyle told me he doesn't have homework, he's only eight. So I asked him to go anyway so that his mom and I could talk. And then I told Jodie about my zip the lip affirmation, but that I felt this wasn't the time for me to zip the lip, because if this was her idea of giving Kyle a chance to escape all our shit, she had a really stupid idea of how to give Kyle a chance to escape all our shit. Then we had one of those arguments where one minute she's screaming that I don't know what I'm talking about, then she's crying on my shoulder, then she's screaming again, and I'm telling her to quiet down because Kyle can hear; and then she's telling me what a great mother she's been, considering; and then she's crying about how she doesn't know what she's doing. And all my detaching with love and zipping the lip is out the window, and

I'm just saying anything I can to get her to calm down, and I promised her something I don't think I should have promised her. Which is that if this thing about the easement comes up again, I will deny that I ever spoke with Mr. Egeberg.

WE ARE ALL ANIMALS!

'm worried about Kyle. I think he's losing touch with his Inner Child. Which I know sounds silly because he's only eight, but I think he's beginning to feel a little overresponsible. And last night he told me he doesn't believe in God. Which is a change. I remember talking to Kyle about God about a year ago, and he kept referring to God as "He," and I told him that God might be a "She" or might not even be like a person. And I remember Kyle saying, "I know that. God is part person and part animal." And I laughed, and then Kyle said, "But mainly animal!" And since then I think about that now and then and it makes me feel good. Because when I walk around in the city and I'm surrounded by people and looking at them hustling around or eating or kissing or arguing or laughing or just scratching themselves, I realize that we're all animals. And that's okay! That's who we are. And we each have to own the animal inside ourselves. Or something like that. The point is, accepting the animal in ourselves doesn't take us farther away from God; it can bring us closer. Okay. Tomorrow I'm taking Kyle to the zoo!

TODAY I WILL ACCEPT THE MESSINESS OF MY LIFE!

Sometimes I look around me, and I just feel dysfunctional. Look at me, I'm sleeping on an air mattress! But then I remember that it's okay. Then I look over at the couch where Kyle is sleeping, and I think that's not okay, and it's hard for me to accept. Then I remember that his mom loves him and he's eating and there's kids starving all over the world, and I start to feel guilty for getting all maudlin about my family. Lighten up, for God's sake, Stuart! Well, today some of the mess looks like it's clearing up. Donnie's lawyer talked to Mr. Egeberg's lawyer and thinks the easement issue will be settled soon. Since Mr. Egeberg died, his lawyer feels that no one in his family will contest our family's claim, which is a big relief to me, since I did promise Jodie I would lie, and I guess now I don't have to. Anyway, Jodie and Kyle will be able to move into Aunt Paula's house within a couple of months. Then Kyle will have his own room, and when I stay with them I can sleep on the couch! But everything won't be perfect. There will still be messes. But that's okay. Because messes are part of life, and they can help us learn and grow. I just thank God this mess with the easement is over!

TODAY I WILL REMEMBER THAT I HAVE MORE TO GIVE IF I TAKE CARE OF ME!

Jodie and I got into a big fight last night because I wanted to take Kyle to an Ala-Tot meeting. (That's Al-Anon for little kids.) She said she doesn't want Kyle to get all immersed in "this alcoholism thing." At one point she even said she wasn't sure Dad is really an alcoholic, which is just bizarre coming from Jodie. In fact, we've been having some pretty bizarre arguments lately, so in the middle of this one, when Jodie went into the kitchen to grab a bag of potato chips, I turned the tape recorder on to record so she could listen to herself later. Well, I just listened to the tape, and do you want to know something weird? I sound horrible! I sound controlling and hysterical and, well, just out of control. At one point I yelled "Listen to me! Listen to me!" twelve times in a row. And when Jodie finally said, "Okay, I'm listening!" I just totally forgot what I was going to say. Well, the first thing I'm going to do today is go to a meeting. And then I'm coming back here and packing and heading on back to Chicago. Because I can't do Kyle any good if I am not a good example. And to be a good example, I think I have to get on with my life, do what I have to do for me, so when I come back I'll be a little stronger and a little better role model.

TODAY I WILL BE OPEN TO THE WONDERMENT OF THIS WORLD! II

When I got on the Greyhound yesterday, I saw this woman sitting by herself. She must have weighed about two hundred and seventy-five pounds. So of course I sat next to her. By the time we got to La Crosse it was pretty clear that she wasn't very open to what I was saying about, you know, program and OA and Higher Power. In fact, she was just kind of mean. Anyway, I just changed seats and sat next to the window and looked out. And you know what? It was spectacular. The leaves were fiery red and friendly orange and bright yellow! I almost went back to the woman to say, "See? There's the Higher Power. Right out there." But I decided to leave it alone. And just enjoy it!

I HAVE SOMETHING TO SAY!

While I was in Minnesota, Julia edited my tape. And she did a terrific job! Actually, she and Steve did a terrific job, because she called him at his advertising agency, and he took what she edited and really glitzed it up with titles and dissolves and all kinds of effects. And I have to tell you, it makes my little cable show look like something from Hollywood! *It's that good!* And it made me realize something. I have something to offer. Because even with all the dissolves and glitz, the true meaning of my show came through. Which is that underneath all the dissolves and glitz of what we show people, we are all human. You know, I am not sure this makes any sense. Anyway, I guess what I'm really saying is that it made me feel good to see a really slick presentation of my show!

WE ARE ALL ANIMALS! II

Steve and Julia slept with each other! While I was gone! He told me last night. Evidently, they really hit it off while editing and went to dinner and started discussing their lives, and well, anyway . . . Steve feels terrible about it, and he added it to his fourth step. Which I guess is the advantage to having your fourth step on computer disc. Steve says he really likes Julia and wants to be her friend, and he's afraid that maybe he'll hurt her, and that maybe he was unconsciously exploiting her attraction to unavailable men. Because he does feel he is unavailable, at least theoretically, since he's still going to marriage counseling twice a week with his wife, though they're still separated. I asked Steve about Donna, the nurse from the National Shame Conference, and Steve told me that she called him to tell him she has a new boyfriend . . . about two days before he slept with Julia! So I asked Steve if he had discussed all this with Julia, and Steve said no, but that he would tonight, and that he's really scared to talk to her about it, and he feels really guilty and ashamed. So I showed him my affirmation on how we are all animals, and I think that made him feel a lot better.

I WILL CELEBRATE MY SUCCESSES!

Julia sold my show! I'm going to be on Lifeline Cable with a five-minute show five days a week!!!!! Can you believe it! They're going to try the show for four weeks, and if they like it . . . who knows. I could be the next John Bradshaw! I am so frightened! But, you know, it's a good kind of fear, because I'm owning my fear, and it isn't stopping me from celebrating my success. Which is just tremendous progress! It used to be that I would dwell on all my failures and be afraid to affirm my successes. Now I, okay, well, I still dwell on my failures, and that's okay, I own the dwelling, but last night I celebrated! Julia and Steve and I went out to a lovely dinner, although they were a little distracted. And why wouldn't they be? Actually, it was kind of cute. They were both trying as hard as they could to keep the focus on celebrating my show, but they kept having these goo-goo eyes for each other. See, Steve told me yesterday that he had his talk with Julia, and they've decided to continue seeing each other but not have sex, but they've decided it's okay if they just make out. I decided I'm glad I'm not still Steve's sponsor, because I would have the hardest time figuring out what to tell him. I did tell him to remember that this is infatuation, not love, and maybe he should put his focus back on trying to work on his marriage. But I don't think he was really listening.

I AM NOT PANICKING!

Okay. I have a week until I tape my first show. And it's very important that I get some sleep between now and then. And worrying about whether I'm going to sleep will not help me sleep. Every night will not be like last night. Sooner or later I will just pass out and get some sleep. Okay. I am panicking. Which is okay. I own my panic. It's *my* panic. Okay. That's good. I can do the show on owning your panic. No, that's just stupid. Okay. I should still write it down on my list of ideas. Let's see, what do I have here? "I Don't Have to Be Paralyzed," "Owning My Fear," "Owning My Insomnia," "Owning My Nausea," "Owning My Panic" . . . Jesus, it's already on the list! I must have written it sometime during the . . . Okay, I'm panicking. But that's okay. I'm owning my own panic.

TODAY I WILL TAKE MY TIME!

Whenever I have something important to do, I start to feel rushed. Even if I have plenty of time. And, of course, when I hurry, I get less accomplished. I think this all stems from my childhood. Whenever there was an opening to get our needs met, it was like a starter's pistol. *Bang!* Better get your needs met *now! This is going to end real soon!* And how about the concept of actually *enjoying* work? Not in the Smalley household. We would let things slide for months, even years, then suddenly Dad would decide that the garage was a mess and needed to be spick-and-span the same night I had to study for a test. Okay. I'm getting upset. I'm sorry. The point is, I have six days to write a five-minute show, and if I just slow down and relax, I'll do just fine. All I have to do is slow down and re . . . okay, I think I know what my first show is!

PROCESS, PROCESS, PROCESS!!!

Process! That's what life is. Process. We always think life is the end result: My show must be a hit. Then I will be respected, and make money, and be loved, and all that crap. That's focusing on the end result. Well, the end result of life is death. Sorry to be negative, but it's true. None of us gets out of here alive. Except maybe there's life after death, but that's not the point. The point is . . . process! Process to me is finding a way to live and a way to work where, instead of driving myself crazy, which I do all the time, instead of that, I actually enjoy myself. I know this is obvious. But as obvious as it is, I find that I don't do it unless I remind myself to do it. So here's a reminder for me and for you. Today, and only today, because it's one day at a time, process, process, process!!! I think I have my second show!

TODAY I FEEL GOOD!

Sometimes I almost have to give myself permission to enjoy feeling good. It used to be that as soon as I realized I was feeling good, I'd start to worry. Uh-oh, I'd think, this isn't going to last. I'd always be waiting for the other shoe to drop. I guess I thought it was my way of steeling myself against disappointments. But it was really a way of robbing myself of happiness. Well, today I feel good! I have my first two shows figured out: "Today I Will Take My Time" and "Process, Process, Process," and I think my third one will be "Today I Feel Good." I'm on a roll! Uh-oh! Now I'm thinking, maybe this is coming too easy and I'm fooling myself. No, you see—that's Stinkin' Thinkin', and exactly what I shouldn't be doing. Anyway, today I'm going down to the studio and meeting with the Lifeline executive to iron out a few details. I feel good!

I AM A FOOL! II

I don't know why I keep thinking things are going to work out for me. Long and short of it, to save money Lifeline wants me to tape twenty shows in one day. That day being the day after tomorrow. I called Julia, and she stormed down to the studio, where she yelled at a young Lifeline executive, which I didn't think was necessary, and neither did Julia, because she made an immediate amends, which I thought was good. Then Julia got on the phone and yelled at the head of programming of Lifeline, who I guess was the woman she had made my deal with. Basically, I get paid per show, so you might think doing twenty in one day wouldn't be so bad. Except that I can't do twenty shows in one day. I'd need twenty ideas, and I only have three, and I'm beginning to think they're pretty stupid. "Process, Process, Process"? Who am I kidding? Anyway, Julia demanded that I shoot only one a day, and the head of programming at Lifeline said no, and Julia looked at me and said I could shoot five in one day but that was it, and the head of programming said no, and Julia told the woman she was going to talk to the CEO of the network, whatever that is, and then Julia hung up. Then Julia tried to call the CEO, but he was in a meeting, and I told Julia to just forget it. It was about noon, and Julia had a lunch appointment, but she offered to skip it and go to an Al-Anon meeting with me. But I lied and told her I had a dentist appointment and bought a case of Sara Lee pound cakes and went home to bed.

TODAY I WILL STAND UP FOR ME!

think Julia would have knocked the door down. Literally. She came straight over when I wouldn't pick up the phone. When I wouldn't let her in, she just kept pounding with her shoulder until the super came up. I think he would have called the police if I hadn't opened the door and let her in. Julia told me she talked to the CEO, who said he'd get into it with the head of programming, but didn't promise anything. Julia said she felt terrible, that she probably should have had a talent agent negotiate for me. I told her we codependents shouldn't use "should." We put enough pressure on ourselves without burdening ourselves with I "should" do this or I "should" have done that. And then I realized that wouldn't be such a bad topic for my show. . . . What show!? Well, Julia called the program director, who said the best she could do was make me tape ten shows in a two-hour taping. Tomorrow. Otherwise the whole deal is off. I immediately started to panic, but I mean real panic. I don't have ten topics. And even if I did, I want the show to be good. I need time. I need . . . I can't do the show under pressure. On the other hand, this is it. This is my chance. You have to take risks in life. It isn't going to be perfect anyway. I can do ten shows if I really concentrate, but relax, and feel good about me. Besides, I already sent some of the money to Jodie. I know, it's a very codependent thing to do, but I just don't want Kyle to have all that pressure to win. Besides, it was only five hundred dollars, which is what I get paid for five shows, and if I tape ten, I get a thousand dollars. So . . . maybe I should just do it. Oh, who am I kidding? If I did ten shows tomorrow, they would suck so bad! Oh, God . . . Anyway, Julia sat me down and looked me square in the eye and said, "You know that there is no possible way for you to do ten shows tomorrow. You'd be taking something great and turning it into garbage. You are a terrific person and you have something terrific to share. Don't let them ruin it. Now, you always stand up for other people. If you can stand up for Kyle, you can stand up for yourself. And when people see that you're standing up for yourself, they respect that, and sure as I am an adult child of an alcoholic, when you tell those people no, they'll give in. Tell them no!" So that's what I did. And I'm waiting to hear their answer. And I'm going out of my gourd.

TODAY I WILL COMPROMISE!

Okay. They did not give in. Julia called yesterday to tell me that the programming director was refusing to budge. Ten shows in two hours. I thanked Julia for a nice try and started to hang up, but I could hear her start to yell on the other end. So we talked some more and Julia told me I had to try it, to look at it as a compromise. After all, we had worked them down from twenty shows in one session. Julia said in life we have to compromise, that sometimes a fear of compromising is just a fear of losing control, control we don't really have anyway. That made a lot of sense to me, but then I remembered what she said the day before about standing up for myself and not letting them ruin my terrific thing, and Julia said that was then, this is now, and that life was about taking risks. So anyway, Julia and Steve and Carl came over last night to help me think of topics, and I think I have ten now, and I have to cut this short because I'm about to go down to the studio and tape these things, and I'm so scared, I'm kind of numb.

ONLY THE MEDIOCRE ARE ALWAYS
AT THEIR BEST!

That's what Andrea said after the taping. She flew in from New York! I did the ten shows in the two hours, which mathematically breaks down to one five-minute show every twelve minutes, which isn't so bad, except that it took them about an hour to light the set, after which I was just freaking out. So just before I went on, Carl, Andrea, Steve, Julia, and I held hands and said the Serenity Prayer. The first show, "Today I Will Own My Panic," went very well and helped calm me down. Carl thought it would make a good first one, because it would be very much "in the now," since I would probably be panicking. The second show, "Today I Will Take My Time," was ironically a little rushed, so I had about thirty seconds at the end with nothing to say, so I did a silent meditation, and I don't think anyone could tell that I was covering up a mistake. And it's okay, because we all make mistakes, that's what makes us human, which was the title of the third show, "We All Make Mistakes, That's What Makes Us Human," which was Steve's idea for a show. I'd say my best show was "Today I Will Show Up," which, if I do say so myself, was magic. Andrea cried. My worst show by far was my last one, called "I Don't Have to Prepare," which was kind of an experiment anyway. You see, I had only settled on nine good topics before I got to the studio, so I got the idea of just winging one of the shows. *Really* do the show "in the now," having nothing prepared. And I just blanked. It was five minutes of me blanking, every once in a while saying something like, "I am blanking now. That's what's going on in the now, right now. Nothing." After a while I slipped into some of the material from "Today I Will Own My Panic," so it wasn't all dead air. After it was over Julia tried to get them to let me do it again, but the studio was booked for a show on boudoir photography, so it was over. That's when Andrea said "Only the mediocre are always at their best." And you know what? I think she's right. I think I was better than mediocre!!

TODAY I WILL BE PATIENT!

Okay. The executives at Lifeline are reviewing the tape today to decide whether to air my show. All I can do is wait. I hate waiting. I'm going nuts. I know I'm just going to sit by the phone all day waiting for Julia's call. Waiting to hear whether all my wants and dreams and life goals are about to be fulfilled or whether they are not. But, see, that's a stupid way to look at this. Stinkin' Thinkin' rearing its ugly head once again. I have to remember that good things will happen to me, whether or not my show is a success. That life is a process and . . . Why don't I believe any of this stuff right now? This is ridiculous. Here I am, agonizing over a show that is supposed to be about telling people how not to agonize. This is a hard business! Why did I choose this anyway? I could have done so many other things. That's not true. I chose this because I never succeeded at anything else. This is it. If I don't get this show, it's over. I'm going to die homeless and penniless; I'm twenty pounds overweight; and no one will ever love me. Okay, that's Stinkin' Thinkin' again. Two Stinkin' Thinkin's this close to each other. I'm in real trouble here. Maybe if I accept my feelings of impatience. Feel my feelings! I'm impatient; I'm frustrated . . . Oh God, please let them put the show on!

TODAY I WILL LET GO OF ANY EXPECTATIONS THAT OTHER PEOPLE WILL BEHAVE LIKE HUMAN BEINGS!!

In Al-Anon maybe the first thing we learn is to let go of our expectations about our alcoholic. Don't expect anything, don't be disappointed. How many times in my childhood was I crushed by my unrealistic expectations of my Dad or my Mom? Then how could I let myself expect to hear from the people at Lifeline? They're probably not drunks (although I don't know!), so naturally I assumed they'd call yesterday. But no, they were probably too busy on their two-hour expense-account lunches to worry about my little show. I'm sorry, but these people have no right to keep torturing me this way. I talked to Carl, and he said that I can't expect these people to understand my feelings. Why not? How hard can it be to figure out my feelings?! Carl said that's not the point, that I'm just torturing myself by expecting them to understand that I'm about to kill myself! In a way I hope they say no, because I don't want to work for people like this.

I LOVE THE PEOPLE I WORK WITH!!

In fact, I love everybody! In Al-Anon, one of the things they say to newcomers is "You may not like us all, but you'll grow to love each of us in a special way." And it's so true. I may not like that the people at Lifeline didn't get back to me right away, but they're people, they're my brothers and sisters, and they're entitled to my love. Oh, by the way, they finally called yesterday. I got the job!!!! Not only are they going to air all ten shows, even the one with me blanking, but they're going to show each one twice a day! I'm going to be helping people twice a day!! And one of the best things I can tell people is to bless the people around you with your love. Oh, and I love you, the reader! Thanks for reading this! I love you!!!!!

STEVE'S WIFE FOUND HIS FOURTH STEP!!!!

We were supposed to have dinner last night, Julia, Steve, and Carl to celebrate. We were all at the restaurant, but Steve didn't show. Finally, we got a call. Steve said he was at his wife's house—his house, too, I guess. Anyway, she had read his fourth step. Evidently Steve's little boy had gotten a new computer, and Steve had come over a couple days ago to put some files from his laptop into the new computer, and I guess accidently one of the files he loaded onto the new computer was his fourth step. Anyway, yesterday, when she was helping her son find a story he had written about the tooth fairy or something, she found this file that said "Fourth Step" and she booted it up and read Steve's fearless moral inventory, which you are supposed to admit to God, yourself, and another human being, but certainly not your wife! When Steve called the restaurant, he sounded kind of scared and, well, sick, I'd say. I asked him if he had any message for Julia, but he just repeated something about being at his home with his wife, and then said good-bye. Julia, Carl, and I spent the whole dinner discussing this new development, although Julia was really kind of quiet, now that I think of it. Carl said he thought it was Freudian, Steve copying his fourth step onto his kid's computer. Carl said that maybe this was good, that it'll bring things to a head between him and his wife. They've been living apart for three months now, maybe now they'd finally break up for good. Then Julia said something strange. She said Steve wants to get back with his wife. And that's why he did this.

I WILL CHOOSE PEOPLE WHO WILL BE THERE FOR ME!

This affirmation is Julia's idea. She says she's always going after unavailable men. Steve really feels awful. He talked to Julia today and told her he's moving back in with his wife and kids. Evidently his wife and he stayed awake all night and did a lot of crying and soul-searching and talking and decided to try to make it work. Actually, Julia says that Steve is probably the most emotionally available man she's ever been involved with. Just the fact that he called her immediately upon breaking up qualified him. Steve's even said he'd like to continue being her friend, and it's even okay with his wife if he sees Julia, you know, for lunch and stuff. She's even invited Julia over for dinner. (That must have been some conversation Steve and his wife had!) But Julia says this isn't about Steve. It's about her. She's thirty-two, wants more than anything to get married and have a family. Why did she get involved with a married man with two kids? Yes, he was separated, and yes, he's a wonderful guy, but . . . Anyway, Julia knows that this is about her father, or fathers, and how she doesn't really trust men to be there for her, or I don't know, how she wants to relive her childhood relationship with men, only this time she'll change the man and make it work out, or I don't know. I don't think Julia really knows either. She told me last night she's thinking of putting a moratorium on sexual relationships for a while. She's always been so quick to jump in bed, she says. Now she thinks it might be time to slow down. I think that might be a good idea. Look how well it's worked for me.

I REFUSE TO FEEL GUILTY! II

Okay. Tonight they're airing my first show. It's at 11:55 P.M., which is okay. The second airing is at 3:45 A.M. It's a twenty-four-hour network and I suppose it could have been worse. Anyway, Carl is throwing a party at his house. About twenty people are invited, including a number of friends from OA and Al-Anon, and Julia, and Andrea is flying in from New York. (I'm beginning to think she makes a lot of money as a book editor. Good for you, Andrea! You deserve it!) Carl invited Steve, too, but he's kind of in a bind. His wife asked if she could come along. She wants to meet me. And he told her Julia would be here, and evidently that's all right with her. And so I called Julia and asked her, and she said that it would be okay with her, too, but she sounded a bit funny. So I realized that even though it would be "okay" with everybody, it would really be uncomfortable. So I told Steve no. Because I want this evening to be about me and my show, and not be ruined by a lot of tension. And normally, I would feel guilty about that. Because I love Steve and want to share this with him. But I—I can't. So I'm sorry, Steve. I really am. But it isn't going to do me any good to feel guilty. So, okay, I'm feeling a little guilty. But that's okay, because I'm owning my guilt. And that's just as good as not feeling guilty. Or almost.

I HAVE FRIENDS! II

I cried last night! Several times. I couldn't believe all the trouble Carl went to. It was an OA feast! Fresh fruit, Rye Krisp, crudités with three types of lo-cal dips!!! It was delicious! And all for me! I looked around at the faces. All my friends. You know how you worry if one set of your friends will like another set? Are they too different to get along? Well, I have to tell you, my Al-Anon friends loved my DA friends, who loved my ACOA friends, who loved my OA friends! And there were about twelve of us from OA, who I'd say among us have lost almost a thousand pounds. That's half a ton! Andrea looked radiant. I'd say she's down to a hundred thirty-five, a hundred and forty tops. And is she ever in top form! She proposed a toast to me and it was so funny that I just started to laugh and cry, and you know what, I can't remember what she said! I think it had something to do with the fact that she was toasting me with low-sodium tomato juice. Anyway, it was beautiful, and I cried! Julia looked a little down, but she was trying not to show it, and she and Andrea started planning a big PR campaign around my book and the show. So I started to cry again. Can you believe this is happening to me? Anyway, as the big moment approached everyone gathered in front of the TV, and this thing came up on the screen, a graphic thing, and an announcer said, "Coming up next, *Daily Affirmations with Stuart Smalley.*" And everybody cheered. Of course, that's when I got scared. What if it sucks? No one will tell me. They'll just look shocked, and then smile and tell me it was great. I had to get up and pace. Then it was 11:55 and I heard the music, then my voice, "I deserve good things! I don't have to beat myself up!" I was watching from the other side of the room. Watching the TV and watching my friends watch the TV. They were smiling. Real, genuine smiles. And as the show continued (They ran "We All Make Mistakes,

That's What Makes Us Human") they were not just smiling, they were nodding in recognition and laughing at a little joke I made, then getting a little misty at some kind of sad things I talked about, then smiling again, then applauding and cheering when the show ended. And then I cried again. I have friends. Good friends! And that says a lot about me!

TODAY I HAVE SOME PERSPECTIVE!

As I watched the show the other night, I started to understand some things about how I do my show. Actually, I'm kind of shocked that I am able to look so clearly at my work, because in the past, I was simply too afraid to look at it at all. First of all, I just watched a tape of the ten shows I taped, and you know what? The people at Lifeline seem to know what they're doing! "We All Make Mistakes, That's What Makes Us Human" was my best show and I'm glad they put it first. And "I Don't Have to Prepare" *is* a disaster and I asked them not to use it. The programming director said, "Fine, you'll just have to tape eleven next time." Which is okay with me; I'm already starting to prepare. You see, when I did my shows for public access, I did them live, which gave me a sense of immediacy. Unfortunately, every two or three shows I would freak out or blank like I did for "I Don't Have to Prepare" and essentially humiliate myself. And now I think that taping a whole bunch in a limited amount of time is a good way to do the show. I don't really have the time to do one over or to try to make it perfect, so the sense of immediacy is still there, and yet I now know that if I totally blow one, I can do it over. It's perfect! And here I was *fighting* it barely a week ago. The long and short of this is, sometimes things become clear in hindsight. And we don't always have perspective as things are happening. And that's okay! As Melody Beattie says in her terrific book *The Language of Letting Go,* "We could strain for hours today for the meaning of something that may come in an instant next year. Now is the time to be. To feel. To go through it. To allow things to happen. To learn. To let whatever is being worked out in us take its course." Isn't that great? I know one thing's clear to me now. I'm going to ask Melody to write the forward to this book. I just hope I can get ahold of her!

STEVE'S WIFE IS TERRIFIC!

Yesterday, Steve called out of the blue and invited me out to dinner with him and his wife. I told him it might be kind of a bad idea because of the book. She might buy the book and then put two and two together and figure out that Steve is Steve. But Steve said she already knows everything in the book and more, and besides, she wanted to meet me. Well, we met, her name's Caroline, and this is one terrific lady! I mean, Steve always said she was a "people pleaser" and that's one of her problems (and mine), but she is a genuinely terrific person. Lively, fun, not what I expected at all. When Caroline went to the ladies' room, Steve looked a little sheepish. He knew what I was thinking, and he said, "You see, isn't she a bitch?"—you know, as a joke. Which is Steve. He told me this was some kind of miracle. That they were getting along great. They've even been having sex! A lot of it. He said it was like everything he had learned in program, everything she had learned in program, and everything they had heard from the marriage counselor, together and individually, had suddenly clicked in. It's like perspective. Sometimes everything becomes clear in an instant. Maybe it helps to be working toward something, which I think in the back of his mind Steve was always doing. When Caroline came back to the table, I decided this time not to watch just her, and started watching them. Steve looked relaxed and happy and kind of relieved.

I CAN ACCEPT HELP FROM PEOPLE!

I have to tape eleven more shows tomorrow. And I think I've got all my topics. I'm replacing "I Don't Have to Prepare" with "I Am Important Enough to Prepare For!" Julia has been very helpful. So much so that I'm beginning to feel a little guilty. I even offered her ten percent of the money I'm being paid. I mean, it's the least I can do, considering she got me the job and negotiated everything for me and came in and saved the whole thing and then got me to do it. And now she's helping to write the thing. I think she deserves at least half. Or more. Actually, if you ask me, she really deserves more than they're paying me. Julia said it would be illegal for her to take ten percent, since she is not legally an agent. And she says she enjoys coming up with topics and ideas. She did seem to be having fun writing the "I Will Not Choose Emotionally Unavailable Lovers" show. Although I changed it a little, because I sensed a little bitterness coming through. Anyway, I talked to Carl about my feeling guilty about Julia's help and he said that was so codependent of me. I'm so used to helping others that I can't accept help myself. And I realized how silly that is. Because I am the world's biggest proponent of program and going to meetings, which, if it's about anything, is about accepting help from others. So, Julia, thank you!

I'M GOOD ENOUGH, I'M SMART ENOUGH, AND DOGGONE IT, PEOPLE LIKE ME! III

I'm doing eleven shows today. They don't have to be perfect. Because you know what? They won't be! But they'll be good! Good enough. Because I'm smart enough! And doggone it, people like me! I'm just going to keep saying that over and over until I believe it.

I FORGIVE JULIA!

No, the shows went great. And Julia was an enormous help. And so was Walter. He's the technical director at the studio. And he really likes my show. He got my set lit in about ten minutes, giving me a lot more time to tape. And everything went smoothly. Julia even wrote down key words on cue cards so I could remember where I was going, but the cue cards were too big and floppy, and Walter copied them over on some smaller cue cards that were a lot easier for Julia to handle. Anyway, at the end of the taping, Walter asked Julia if she was married or was seeing anybody, because he was interested in asking her out. Now, Walter's not the world's most handsome guy, but he's presentable, and really nice and really smart. So when Julia said that yes, she was seeing someone, I was doubly surprised. And on the way back when I admonished her for lying, Julia said, "What did you want me to tell him? 'No, I'm not married and I'm not seeing anybody, but I would never go out with you because you've got a big nose, a bad haircut, and you're the technical director of a little rinky-dink TV studio.' " And I said, "But he's a great guy. Maybe the reason you aren't immediately attracted to him is that he's emotionally available." And Julia said, "Please! And anyway, I told you I was putting a moratorium on sexual relationships." And I said, "So, he didn't ask you to have sex with him." And Julia said, "Oh, c'mon! That's all men want." And we talked some more, and Julia told me she'd never gone out with a man more than once and not had sex. So I told her that maybe that was her and not the men, and that maybe she could date without having sex. And then she said she couldn't believe she was listening to me lecture her on sex and relationships, and she said, "Look at you. How long has it been since you've been in a relationship? When did you leave your rage-aholic? Three years ago? When was the last time you went on a date, Stuart? I mean, c'mon, you're pathetic." I don't know which was worse. That Julia didn't make an immediate amends or that what she said was true. And you want to know the oddest thing? The other night when I had dinner with Steve and his wife, I had this sick thought flash through my mind that maybe I'd run into Dale somewhere and we'd look into each other's eyes and the magic would be there again, and we could be like Steve and Caroline. Is that sick or what? At any rate, I don't blame Julia. I think she's still upset about Ste— Oh, there's the phone. . . . Hello? . . . Oh, hi . . . No, that's okay. I understand. . . . No, really. It's okay. . . . Well, I'm doing it right now. . . . Well, I was talking about it. . . . Okay, I'll put it in. . . . No, it belongs in. Look, I'll call you back. . . . Love you. Bye . . . That was Julia. She wanted you to know she made an amends.

I'VE BEEN SUBPOENAED! II

This is a nightmare! You remember that after Mr. Egeberg died, in a moment of weakness I promised Jodie I would lie about talking with Mr. Egeberg, if it ever came up again. And then soon after, much to my relief, Donnie's lawyer called Mr. Egeberg's lawyer, who said that now that Mr. Egeberg was gone, the family would sell the easement for the original three thousand dollars. Are you with me? Anyway, it turns out that before he died, Mr. Egeberg, who was a widower with no kids, had discussed this with his nephew or niece, I'm not sure, named Merle Egeberg. And Merle Egeberg is refusing to sell my family the easement, because he/she says his/her uncle *did* talk to me. Well, my family has now gone ahead and petitioned the probate court for an allowance of their claim. In other words, once again they want me to lie. Oh, God, I can't believe I'm going through this one more time. It's like Yogi Berra said: "It's déjà vu all over again." Except this feels very sick. There was something I once heard in an Al-Anon meeting about the difference between a healthy person and a sick person. If there's a hole in the street, the healthy person might fall into it once, but from then on, he always avoids the hole and goes around it. But the sick person keeps falling in. Promising Jodie I'd lie was like falling into the hole again. Maybe if I just call this Merle Egeberg, I could explain everything. But that would blow my family's case wide open. Donnie's lawyer says that Merle can't testify about what his/her uncle told him/her. It would be inadmissable, because it's hearsay. We have an airtight case. Unless I talk.

THIS TIME, NOBODY'S GETTING IN HERE!!

Joanne might say that the Higher Power doesn't want me to give the deposition. You see, I got on the plane to Minneapolis and I fell asleep. Because I had been up all night trying to figure out what to do. So I fell asleep. And I guess while we were in the air, Minneapolis was hit with about twenty inches of snow, and we couldn't land. We had to go back to Chicago. But I was asleep, you see. And then someone was shaking me, telling me to put my seatback in an upright position. It was the flight attendant. Dale! That's right! Dale! No, I wasn't imagining it. Dale, my rage-aholic ex, is a flight attendant for Northwest. So anyway, when I heard Dale's voice, I thought I was having a nightmare, and I screamed. Then Dale shook me a little harder, and I guess I didn't wake up and Dale started yelling at me to get up. Which is something Dale always did when we were living together, because I think at the time I was hard to get up because sleep was my only sanctuary. So when I heard Dale yelling I started to scream some more. When I finally woke up, everyone was looking at us. But I was still half asleep, and when I asked where we were, Dale said we were landing in Chicago and for some reason I said, "You're lying!" and Dale just started screaming at me! In front of everyone! It was the most humiliating thing that has ever happened to me in my life. My rage-aholic ex screaming at me thirty thousand feet above Lake Michigan. By the time we landed I was almost comatose, practically in a fetal position. I fell into a cab, stopped at a Henny Penny and picked up a couple of cases of Animal Crackers, then came straight home and into bed. The phone's unplugged, the door's locked, and nobody's coming in!

I WILL OBEY THE LAW!

I guess one of my big heroes outside the recovery movement would have to be Dr. Martin Luther King, Jr. Some of my program friends say he was a grandiose womanizer, but I think he was a great man, a great leader, and a great teacher. One of the things he taught was civil disobedience, which I guess he got from Gandhi, who Joanne once told me had a food disorder, but you know what? I'm beginning to think Joanne is just a big idiot. I'm sorry, that was judgmental. Joanne, if you're reading this, I make an amends. It's just that I'm in a real state right now. I'm on a plane (United), flying to Minneapolis. There's a hearing, not a trial, tomorrow, and . . . Oh, I'm sorry. The last five days. I'm sure you want to know about the last five days. Well, I took to my bed on the 30th, and I guess all my friends figured I was in Minneapolis, so no one came by to get me, which made me even more depressed. Then on the night of the 31st I heard the doorbell and just yelled "Go away!" and a few minutes later the bell rang again, and I yelled again, and so on and so on, and I'm sure you figured out by now that it was Halloween, which is normally my favorite holiday, and I guess a number of trick-or-treaters egged my door. And, well, a couple days later the eggs started to smell, and one of the neighbors called the police. When the police came by and demanded that I open the door, I told them I didn't have to. And they said I did have to for some legal reason that sounded pretty convincing. So I said I was practicing civil disobedience, protesting for the right of a de-pressed person to stay in bed. Which I still think is something worth fighting for. That's when the policeman called Carl, who I guess had left his number with the precinct in case anything like this happened. Well, Carl must have known how serious this one was, because he shamed me right away. "This is attention-get-ting behavior, Stuart!" And I guess he was right. Or I don't know. Anyway, I got up and let Carl in and plugged the phone back in, and it rang almost immediately. And it was Jodie saying I had to get up here for this hearing, and that I had to lie. Which is breaking the law and has nothing to do with civil disobedience. And I asked Carl what I should do, and after talking it through he told me I had to make the decision myself.

TODAY I WILL PRAY FOR KNOWLEDGE OF HIS WILL! (OR HERS!)

My family is treating me like they really love me. Which just makes me sick. Because it means they want something from me. Jodie's the most devious, and the most effective. She thanked me for sending the money for Kyle's swimming and showed me a trophy he'd won and told me Kyle's coach says he's swimming even faster now that there isn't so much pressure on him. Then she showed me a note from Kyle's teacher saying what a smart child he is and how she thinks Kyle will do even better in school if he has his own bedroom with a desk and lamp where he can study. It made me think of those damn lamps Dad made with his wine bottles. Okay, I'm sorry, I'm getting upset. Anyway, we all went out to lunch with Donnie's lawyer. He told me the judge accepted Donnie's lawyer's explanation about my missing the depositions: I was on the plane, which I was (I had the boarding pass); we couldn't land, which we couldn't; then I got sick, which I did. I was also incommunicado for five days because I pulled the phone jack out of the wall, but he didn't get into that. Anyway, the hearing's today, in about an hour. Donnie's lawyer told me I might not even get called. The Egeberg family lawyer will probably just assume I'd lie. But if I do get called, it's absolutely vital that I keep my promise to Jodie, that I say I never talked to Orville Egeberg. That's all I have to say, and my family gets the easement, and Jodie can move into Aunt Paula's house, and Kyle gets his own room, and everybody else gets about ten thousand dollars, minus what we owe Donnie's lawyer. If I tell the truth, not only doesn't that stuff not happen but every other member of my family could be prosecuted for giving false testimony under oath in their depositions. What if we all just tell the truth tomorrow, I said, you know, and throw ourselves on the mercy of the court? Then

Jodie started crying, and Dad yelled at me and said that we'd never be in this mess if I hadn't come up here in the first place and tried to fix everything. And of course, he's right. I got everybody into this. Now somebody please tell me, how do I get us out?

TODAY I WILL REMEMBER THAT ALCOHOLISM IS A CUNNING, BAFFLING, POWERFUL DISEASE! IV

I'll probably never see my family again. Unless I'm called back for the perjury trial. Although the judge seems to think my testimony at the hearing will be sufficient. I'm thinking now that maybe I could have made things easier for everybody if I had just told them I knew all along I was going to tell the truth. But I honestly didn't. My Higher Power said to just do what I thought was right at the time, and even when they called my name I didn't know what I was going to do. And Donnie's lawyer sure made it hard for me. At the beginning of the hearing he called Jodie, then Donnie, then Dad, and they all told their part of the "story." And as they were doing it, they would sneak a glance at me, as if saying, "See, this is easy." And it did look easy. The Egebergs' lawyer wasn't exactly Perry Mason, and the courtroom wasn't even a courtroom. It was like a dingy conference room with low ceilings and bad fluorescent lighting. But when I got up there and the judge gave me the oath, "Do you swear to tell the truth, the whole truth, and nothing but the truth *so help you God?*" Well . . . I didn't cry or get emotional. I just told the truth, and I tried to explain how I was at fault because of my codependent need to fix everything, and that this was really about alcoholism, but the judge kept cutting me off and telling me to just answer the questions. At one point Donnie's lawyer made an objection and said that I was insane, but Jodie, who was already crying, just broke down and admitted that everything I said was true, and then Dad hit her— Oh, I'm sorry. . . . Sure, I'll have the peanuts; in fact, do you have a couple extra bags? . . . Anyway, I'm on the plane (United) home, and . . . Reese's peanut butter cups! That's it. I'll grab a crate of those on the way home.

THIS TOO SHALL PASS! III

Carl anticipated everything. Somehow he found out what plane I was on and was waiting for me at my door. I told Carl not to bother, I was going to go to bed with the Reese's cups. But Carl said I couldn't. I had to tape more shows. Evidently, the Lifeline switchboard was getting lots of calls for "more Stuart," and they want to extend my contract for thirteen weeks! Wouldn't you know it? At the low point of my life, something good like this would happen to spoil it. Anyway, we took the crate of Reese's cups and donated them to a drug and alcohol rehab on the South Side.

I AM ENTITLED TO GOOD REPRESENTATION!

Lifeline wants to renegotiate my contract. Fortunately, the deal Julia made with them only gives them options on my show for two more thirteen-week periods. Now they want options for four years! At one hundred fifty dollars per show. That's seven hundred and fifty dollars a week! For four years! That's one hundred and fifty thousand dollars! I could buy Jodie and Kyle a house with that! But Julia said that they would just have the *option* of keeping me on for four years. They could drop me whenever they wanted. Oh. Well, what should I do? I asked. She said, "Fire me." Which meant that I should get a real agent. A good one. In the past, just the thought of asking someone to represent me made me feel very small. For some reason, whenever I go to anyone, a dentist, a doctor, a lawyer, I feel like I'm lucky they've agreed to see me. And whatever they say goes. So I'm going to do what I did before when I picked that lawyer in Minneapolis, Arnie. . . . Jesus, why didn't I go back and ask Arnie about the hear— Okay, you see, I have to get professional advice. Okay. I'm going to go to three different agents, and interview them, and I will be the one in charge. I don't have to hire any of them. I'm the boss! . . . I think I'll ask Julia to come along.

TODAY I WILL NOT TRUST AGENTS!

That's what one of the agents said. After viewing my tape, he said I should use it as an affirmation. His name is Marty, and he's a very big agent here in Chicago. I liked him right away and so did Julia. I think it's because he really seems to understand what I'm doing, but he's not in program or anything. It's like he has a dispassionate enough view of the whole thing while still getting it. He even suggested I try to market a little talking affirmation doll of myself. When you pull the string it, or I, says "I am good enough!" or "I make good decisions" or "I don't have to eat that piece of cake." I told him I thought that might be a bit tacky, but Julia said, "I am entitled to merchandise myself," and we all laughed. I didn't like the other two agents as much. One was Susan, who my book agent recommended, who said she was in OA, but I think she's gone like maybe twice in her life, but pretended to know all about it. The other agent was Colin. He's British, and neither Julia nor I trusted him because he said, "The one thing you should know about me is that I never lie." So, we're going with Marty.

TODAY I WILL REMEMBER THAT ALCOHOLISM IS A CUNNING, BAFFLING, POWERFUL DISEASE! V

Today's Veterans Day. Dad's a veteran, but he doesn't ever march in the parades or anything. In fact, he never really talks about the service, except to say that the guys who do the most talking probably never saw battle. Mom told me once that Dad was in the Battle of the Bulge, and his unit got ambushed by some Nazis, and he was the only guy in the unit who survived. They really don't know what causes alcoholism. Some say that it's all genetic; some say growing up in a dysfunctional environment can make you more susceptible; or maybe some horrible traumatic event can trigger it. At any rate, my Uncle Pete once told me that when he got back from the war, Dad had trouble sleeping, and had bad dreams, and that before the war he never had trouble with John Barleycorn. Of course, Uncle Pete used to lie a lot.

TODAY I CAN TURN IT OVER!

I have to tape ten more shows tomorrow. And you'd think this time I'd be less nervous. Which I am. I am a little less nervous. But barely. I keep thinking of reasons I should be nervous. Marty's coming to the taping. That's a crazy reason to be nervous. He's working for me. But I think mainly I'm making myself nervous because the Lifeline people are talking about renegotiating. If these shows are bad, maybe they'll change their minds. And then I'm thinking maybe if these shows are great, Marty can get me some kind of bonus for signing and I can pay Merle Egeberg whatever for the easement and Jodie and Kyle can move in, and maybe I can bribe the judge not to prosecute Dad and Donnie for perjury. How's that for putting pressure on yourself! Okay. I am turning this all over to H.P. and just getting on with what I have to do right now, today. Which is come up with ten topics. How about, "Today I Don't Have to Think of Reasons to Make My Life More Difficult!"?

I AM THE BEST AT WHAT I DO!

Marty said all my shows were terrific. So did Walter. In fact, I think I'm going to insist in my renegotiation that Walter always be the technical director when I tape. Julia thought this batch wasn't as good as the first two, but I think she's still in the dumps about Steve. Did I say Marty thought the shows were great? Because he did. He made a good suggestion too. After the first one, entitled "Today I Will Be Humble," Marty pointed out that the show works best when I tell stories about my own experiences. For instance, in "Today I Will Be Humble" I told about how I'm getting very critical of Joanne's spirituality to the point where I find that I'm judgmental when she shares in meetings, and yet the other day Joanne said something that just hit me like a ton of bricks. She said, "The most intimate relationship you can have is with yourself." And I thought that's really beautiful, and the whole experience reminded me that I need to be more humble and be open to messages from . . . wherever. Anyway, Marty thought that was great. And he suggested putting just a little more of myself in each of the shows, and Julia said something like, "That's impossible," because I think she was a little jealous of Marty. And quite frankly she was not being humble. She was not really open to Marty's suggestions. Anyway, the shows were my best ever. I am good at this!!

I AM ENTITLED TO AS MUCH AS I CAN GET!

Marty thinks we should play hardball with Lifeline. And why not? They're certainly not above playing hardball with me. I mean, that's free-market capitalism, and it's a good system, as the fall of the Soviet Union I think proves. I deserve good things! And so does my family! Well . . . *Kyle* deserves good things. And the rest of them, too, I guess. But this is about me. Me and my DA issues. I mean, you should see the hole I live in. I don't even have a car! Marty thinks that the last batch of shows is so strong, we could scare the bejeezes out of Lifeline. He's talking syndication. That's right. Syndication! Like Oprah! Can you believe it? Marty says we tell Lifeline that we will take the show to a syndicator if they don't give me a thousand a show! Also, we demand better time slots (which considering the strength of the show is obviously no problem), more on-air promo, 100 percent of all merchandising, et cetera et cetera. I mean, *I'm helping people!*

TODAY I TRUST MY OWN JUDGMENT.

Growing up in a dysfunctional home can cause you to lose faith in your own judgment. Everything's crazy. One moment Dad is grumpy and telling you to get out of his hair; then a little while later he's had something to drink and suddenly he's promising you a new bike; then the next day he's forgotten all about the bike, and if you bring it up, he tells you you're crazy! Actually that never happened to me; my Dad never promised me a new bike when he was drunk *or* sober, but I've heard this example a lot, so I thought I'd use it. Anyway, in an alcoholic home, you stop believing in your own ability to assess reality, and that's why we codependents so often rely on other people's judgment and not our own. That's why I'm going to trust my judgment about this last batch of shows, and not Julia's and not Carl's. Carl saw the tape and said that something happened between like the second show and the fifth or so, where it was like I was too confident or something. So I looked at the shows again, and you know what? I think they're great! And so does Marty. But that doesn't matter. What matters is *my* opinion. And I agree with Marty that these new shows are great and that we should really sock it to Lifeline in this renegotiation. And Marty really thinks the merchandising could be significant. He has this incredibly great idea: 1-900-THAT'S OK!

TODAY I WILL LET GO OF FEAR!

The Lifeline people saw my new shows, and they told Julia they didn't like them as much as the previous ones. Marty thinks they're just saying that to scare me because of this renegotiation. If that's the case, it worked! Suddenly I'm afraid that the shows are no good, that Carl and Julia are right, that I don't know what I'm doing, that they're going to cancel the show, and I'm going to die homeless and penniless and no one will ever love me. Okay. We know what that is. Stinkin' Thinkin'! And I've decided that Stinkin' Thinkin' is just fear. So today I refuse to be crippled by fear! And right now I am asking my Higher Power to take my fear away, because as they say, "Courage is fear that has said its prayers." Okay. I feel better. My shows are good! They're better than good. They're great! And I'm just going to tell Marty to do whatever he thinks is best.

I MAKE GOOD DECISIONS!

Julia called me yesterday to complain about Marty. And it was very upsetting. She said Marty had told the programming director at Lifeline to talk to him, not Julia, about my shows. So I called Marty, and told him I was upset. And he said that was just the point. He said he didn't want Julia upsetting me like she did the other day when she told me the executives at Lifeline didn't like my new shows. He said he's had a lot of experience interpreting what these executives are saying, and that he thinks it's better if he acts as a buffer between me and the network. I called Julia back and she got angry, not just at Marty but at herself. Maybe she'd been helping me too much, enabling me in a way. She said I don't need a buffer, that I should be talking to the programming director myself. Then I called Marty, and he said that was ridiculous, that the whole point of having an agent is to have someone who can be tough with the executives so that the artist, that's me, can maintain a friendly relationship with them. And that seemed to make a lot of sense to me, because I thought back to Roz Weinman and how much better it might have been to have someone else take all that abuse from her. So I decided that Marty was making sense and he does have more experience at this than Julia . . . so I told Marty that he should be the one to deal directly with the programming director, *but* that I wanted him to keep Julia apprised of everything that's going on. And he said that, of course, he would. Pretty good solution, huh?!

I'M GOING TO BE CARL'S BEST MAN!

Carl and Andrea finally set the date. The wedding is December 29th, here in town. And I'm the best man! Marty thinks Carl asked me because I'm becoming such a big star. But I don't believe that for a second.

TODAY I WILL LET GO AND LET GOD!

I asked Marty how the renegotiation is going, and he said it looks very good, but he doesn't want me to get into the day to day back and forth. I'd go crazy. And he's right. It's so nice to be able to let go and let . . . Gee, I almost said "Let go and let Marty." Isn't that funny!? I should really tell Carl and Julia. Oh, Julia called me 'cause she wanted to know what was happening, so I told her to call Marty but that she really shouldn't have to, because Marty is supposed to keep her apprised of everything. And she said she had called Marty, but he didn't return her call. So I called Marty and he said that he had tried her back, but he missed her. And then I called Julia and she said that was impossible because her secretary is always there, and then she tried Marty while I was on the other line, but evidently, he was in a meeting. So I tried Marty a little later, but he was in a meeting again, and I left word for him to call Julia. Anyway, I've got to find out when they want me to tape more shows. I hope it's not the 22nd. That's my birthday! And I'd rather celebrate than work. So I guess I should call Marty. Gee, maybe Marty would like to throw me a little impromptu birthday party!

T.HIS H.URT I. N.OW K.NOW!

Carl came over today. I thought it was to discuss my duties as best man or maybe plans for my birthday. But he really wanted to talk to me about Marty. He told me Andrea has been reading the new pages and is kind of concerned about me. Concerned about *me?* I said. I'm doing great! My show's a hit! People are asking for "more Stuart." It's obvious that I am touching lives and really making a difference. I mean, how many people can say that about themselves? And Carl said a lot of people could. Teachers and nurses and social workers, and fathers and mothers and construction workers, and telephone operators, and the guy who drives the Zamboni at the ice rink, and . . . And I said, okay, what's your point? And Carl said that he was wondering if I wasn't getting a little grandiose. And if Marty wasn't feeding this grandiosity a little bit. Or a lot. I thanked Carl, and I told him that I really had to think about this. So Carl left and I decided to sit down and think. And then I looked over the pages I had faxed Andrea. And I reread the one from two days ago, where Marty said that he thought Carl asked me to be best man because I was becoming such a big star. And I think that maybe Carl was hurt by that, and understandably is angry with Marty for thinking that. But instead of taking it all out on Marty, Carl took it a little out on me by accusing me of grandiosity. And I think that might be misdirected anger. Because maybe Carl is just a bit angry at himself. Because maybe what Marty said is just a little true. And that hurts. But it's okay. I forgive Carl.

E.ase G.od O.ut!

I still don't know when I'm going to tape my next batch of shows, but it has to be soon. The other night they repeated one of my first shows, "We All Make Mistakes, That's What Makes Us Human." I guess there must have been a lot of requests for it. Anyway, Julia asked me to coffee after last night's Al-Anon meeting, I thought to discuss plans for my birthday tomorrow, but she wanted to talk to me about Marty. She says she and Marty are playing phone tag, but he only calls her office at 7:30 in the morning or at night, so she's convinced he's trying to avoid her. I told her he just must be very busy. Because the last couple days *I've* been having a hard time getting ahold of Marty to find out when I'm taping next, which I have to admit is making me a little crazy. Julia wants me to call the programming director to tell her to let Julia talk to her about what's going on with my renegotiation. So I told her I'd call Marty about that, and Julia got really angry. In fact, she said, "I am really angry with you, Stuart." Which is very healthy. And then she said she thought that the whole last month with what happened with Dale and especially what happened in Minnesota has made me very fragile, and that in my weakness I had let Marty appeal to my ego. And then she reminded me of the program saying, ego: *E*ase *G*od *O*ut. And she said I had made Marty my Higher Power, and that it was time I snap out of this. And then I told her that she shouldn't take my inventory. And then she said that I'm being an asshole, and that that's okay, she loves me anyway, but that she was afraid I was going to get hurt. And then she told me she was going to talk to the CEO and ask him what was going on and she didn't need my permission or Marty's. And then I said, Look who's being grandiose, and she said— Ooops, there's the phone. . . . Hello? . . . Oh, hi, I was just talking about you. You want to make an amends? . . . Bad news? . . .

I AM A FOOL! III OR IV (WHO CARES?)

I can't even keep track of how big a fool I am. In case you haven't guessed, I lost my show. Julia thinks Marty was looking for a quick score. If he could make a lot of money real quick with me, then I was worth dealing with. But . . . Oh, why even go into it? The point is, I don't deserve a show. I mean, it is ridiculous, a diseased person like me telling people how to run their lives! I mean, it's almost funny. I'd laugh if I were someone else. And the worst part is, everything Julia and Carl have said is true: I've been a grandiose asshole! I am so ashamed! I knew Carl and Julia and Steve would rush right over, so I threw some things in a bag, bought about twenty boxes of Nabisco Nilla Wafers, and got this room at the Motel 6. They'll never find me here. This is the absolute low point. *And on my birthday!* That's right. November 22nd. The day they shot Kennedy. I've never felt that it was more fitting.

I AM LOVED UNCONDITIONALLY!

I really have incredible respect for the Chicago police. No, they're not the ones who love me unconditionally. My friends do. But the police found me. Pretty quickly, in fact. Carl contacted the precinct, and they checked all the motels along the bus route from the Henny Penny, which is where I get my sweets. Carl disguised his voice and said he was the maid, and I told him/her to go away. But then Carl said they'd fire him/her if he/she didn't keep the room clean, and that his/her husband who drinks a lot would probably beat him/her. So I opened the door. I was so embarrassed when I saw it was Carl. Mainly because of the way I'd acted in the last week or so, but also because he had fooled me so easily. I told Carl to go away, but of course, he wouldn't. He told me he loved me unconditionally, and that it didn't matter how grandiose I had been, or how big an asshole, that it was okay! Nobody's perfect. We all make mistakes, that's what makes us human. I told Carl it sounded so hollow. Carl said that that was because he was saying it, not me, that I was born to carry the message to others. And I said yeah, right! That's why I can't keep my stupid little show on the air. And then he told me that Julia got it back for me. She talked to the people at Lifeline and got me another chance. I just sat on the bed crying; I just don't deserve this. Carl told me Julia wanted me to come over to her place to discuss details about the show, but I said I couldn't, I was too embarrassed. And then Carl said that I had to go, that on top of being grandiose, did I also want to be ungrateful? So Carl drove me over to Julia's, where my friends were waiting to surprise me. It's funny. In what I now call my Grandiose Period (November 13–21), I had all these expectations about what my friends would do for my birthday. But now in one of my many Shame Spiral Periods I had none. So was I surprised! Everyone was there. Even Joanne and Bob (they're back together) and Steve and Caroline, his wife. (When Julia invited them, Steve asked her if it would make her uncomfortable, and Julia said she wasn't sure, but that she wouldn't have invited them if she didn't want them to come, so they came.) And I don't think anyone was uncomfortable. In fact, we had a great time! Andrea couldn't be there, but she did send me a great birthday present. A mock-up of the book cover. With a picture of me, and in big type, "I'm good enough! I'm smart enough! And doggone it, people like me!"

TODAY I WILL LIVE ONE MINUTE AT A TIME!

I tape ten more shows the day after tomorrow. Fortunately, I wrote a few during my Grandiose Period. But frankly, after all the drama of the last couple days, it's nice to just settle down and do what I have to do, one day at a time, one hour at a time, one minute at a time, one second at a time. Better one minute at a time. One second at a time is just too confusing. Anyway, in the next minute I'm going to stop doing this and move on to my show. So that's what I'm doing this very minute. Right now.

I AM AN ADULT!

Evidently Marty had created a little bad blood between me and Lifeline, especially the program director. Julia thinks she's smoothed things over, but I've decided that I should really talk to this woman myself and get to know her and let her know me and discuss the show and what she likes and doesn't like and what I'd like to do with the show myself. It's the adult thing to do. Oh, and speaking of the adult thing to do, yesterday I officially fired Marty. Actually, I think he had fired me, because he wouldn't return my calls, but I called anyway. He was in a meeting, so I faxed him a letter terminating our professional relationship. That felt good. It's good to be an adult. As long as you keep the child within you alive. Which is why after I meet with the program director later today, I'm going bowling with Julia and Steve and Caroline and their kids. Evidently, Julia and Caroline really hit it off. Actually, that's a little too adult for me, but hey, it's not my life! Oh, and I tape tomorrow. I've got eight shows figured out, and I should be able to finish the other two this morning. Is that adult or what!?

TODAY I FEEL GOOD! II

Not bad! It's November 26th, and I've already felt good twice this year! That's just a little joke. But it's true, I do feel good. Julia says it's because I'm learning from my mistakes. And I am! I talked with the programming director, Mary. And she's great. She had her little baby at her office, and at one point the baby was crying, so she had to excuse herself and breastfeed, so I went out and read a magazine. It was called the *Hollywood Reporter* and it's a show-business magazine and it happened to have a list of agents in Chicago. So I xeroxed the list, and I've decided to get a new agent who will handle the business side of this thing. But I will keep in constant touch with Mary, who I think genuinely likes my show, especially the first batch I did, and I think she'll like what I'm taping today. My first show is entitled "Alcoholism, a Three-fold Disease: Thanksgiving, Christmas, and New Year's!" which is an old Al-Anon or AA joke. Steve says alcoholism is a *four*-fold disease, Thanksgiving, *Hanukkah*, Christmas, and New Year's. That's what I love about Steve. His amazing sense of humor! And generosity! He said I could use his joke in the show. Anyway, the point of the show is that this time of year can be very difficult for recovering people. I know that I'm a little concerned about this Thanksgiving, which is the day after tomorrow. Steve and Caroline asked me what I was doing, and I really don't know. Usually I go home. But, of course, I'm a persona non grata in Minnesota, especially with Dad and Donnie. But that's okay! I have detached from that situation with love. I feel good. And I'm going to do ten great shows!!!!!!!!!!!

DAD SHOT DONNIE!

After I finished taping my last show, Julia came running up to me. From the look on her face, I thought I had done a really awful show. But as soon as she told me, I forgot about the show, I forgot about everything. It was like I was in a bad dream. Jodie was on the other end of the control room phone, hysterical. Dad shot Donnie, she kept saying. Dad shot Donnie. Where? In the side! I mean where, in the house? In the side! In the side! With what? His deer rifle! Dad shot Donnie with his deer rifle! Why? What happened? Dad shot Donnie! Is Donnie okay? No, Dad shot him! In the side! I mean, is Donnie going to live? I don't know! Dad shot him! I couldn't get Jodie to calm down. And this is a person who lives for crises. So I told Jodie I was coming home, first plane. And I called my parents' house, and got Mom's voice on the phone machine saying she was at the hospital. So I called the hospital and asked for Donnie's room, and the phone rang and Donnie picked it up! And he told me what happened. He and Dad were deer hunting. And, of course, they were drinking. A lot. And they ran out of beer. So Donnie went off to buy some, and when he came back with the case of beer, Dad thought he was a deer and shot him. Well, at least I'm home for Thanksgiving!

THAT ATTITUDE OF GRATITUDE, IT'S NOT JUST A PLATITUDE!

Donnie looked pretty good yesterday. A little pale. But he's going to be all right. Dad was kind of embarrassed. And he didn't give me any trouble about the Egeberg hearing. If he had, I might have said something about how rarely you see a deer carrying a case of beer, especially one wearing an orange hat. Mom seemed all confused. Mainly about how this would affect Thanksgiving dinner. And Jodie still seems a little hysterical. She brought Kyle to the hospital, but didn't want him to see Grandpa, whom she now considers a violent degenerate. So Kyle just kind of sat around the hospital cafeteria waiting till it was time for his swimming practice. I had to get some air after a while, so I went to this Al-Anon meeting near the hospital, and it was one of the most beautiful I've ever gone to. Since it was the day before Thanksgiving, the speaker, a sweet, pretty girl named Erin, talked on the topic of "gratitude." Erin told a story about how one day in high school she was chosen to be on the cheerleading squad. She said that she was so happy she literally started skipping home, running and jumping with joy through the woods toward her house. Only, as she got closer to home, she stopped running and slowed down, realizing that there was no one in her home that she could share her good news with. She said it was like her home was dark and heavy, covered with black clouds. In her home no one could celebrate. And you could never be grateful for anything good. Just guilty. So she didn't tell anyone in her home that she had been chosen for cheerleader. Erin spoke so clearly and simply and straight from the heart that it set the tone for the whole meeting, and everybody's share was just beautiful. I talked about how grateful I was to be there and how grateful I was that my big brother is still alive.

TODAY I WILL REMEMBER THAT ALCOHOLISM IS A CUNNING, BAFFLING, POWERFUL DISEASE! VI

Thanksgiving this year was pretty eerie. Jodie refused to come over to Mom and Dad's. So with Donnie in the hospital, and Aunt Paula in heaven, it was just the three of us. Me, Mom, and Dad. That didn't stop Mom from making a fifteen-pound turkey with all the trimmings. She kept herself busy cooking all morning, and Dad got drunk early, so I went over to visit Donnie. It was the first time we had been alone. Donnie told me that Dad had tried to sneak him a pint bottle of Jack Daniel's on Wednesday. But that he told Dad he didn't want it, and Dad got mad. Donnie said that the shooting was a blessing. It scared the shit out of him, he said. And he realized he has to stop drinking and drugging. This is it, he said. I told Donnie about Erin at the Al-Anon meeting and how I had shared that I was grateful he was still around. Donnie started to cry, and I thought it was because he was moved by what I said, but it wasn't. He said he was worried about Dad. I guess things have gotten worse lately. I told Donnie my dream, about catching Dad when he falls off the roof. And then Donnie said we have to save Dad. We have to do an intervention. We have to make Dad get help. I said I don't know. I think people get help when they're ready for help. So I told Donnie I'd think about it. And when I got home, Dad was passed out in front of the Lions-Bears game, and Mom and I sat down to dinner alone.

TODAY I KNOW WHAT I HAVE TO DO!

Jodie is in favor of the intervention. I felt I had to discuss it with her before I talked to Mom. If I couldn't convince Jodie, Mom would be impossible. In fact, I asked her to talk to Mom, but she said they're not really speaking right now. Something about a test Kyle was supposed to take to qualify for a scholarship to some private school with a swimming pool. At the last minute one of them lost the directions and Kyle was late for the test, and they each blame the other. I think that's it. Anyway, Jodie thinks that it would probably be most effective for Donnie to talk to her. And I think that's a pretty smart idea, considering where he is and how he got there. Jodie is a lot smarter than anyone gives her credit for. It's just that lately, she's awfully nervous. For example, she freaks out if you talk about any of this in front of Kyle. Like he doesn't know! So Donnie's talking to Mom later today, and I'm calling professionals who organize interventions. It's weird. I feel like this is the right thing to do. But I feel kind of guilty. So I called Carl. He told me to go back to the hospital and ask Donnie if he feels guilty.

DENIAL AIN'T JUST A RIVER IN EGYPT!

I know Dad knows he has a problem. And I know that he's in denial about it too. That's the way it works, I guess. The one thing for sure is that Dad would fight tooth and nail against any threat to his drinking. Still, Joe says that almost 90 percent of all interventions work; when finally faced with their loved ones, their friends, and very often the loss of their livelihood, alcoholics will usually give in. And more often than not, the alcoholic is actually relieved. Joe's the Employee Assistance Program director at the place Jodie works or used to work, a medical testing laboratory. Jodie's back went out last year from always bending over her work, and Joe was very helpful in getting Jodie her disability, so we ended up asking him to run the intervention. Donnie gets out of the hospital today, and we're all going down to Joe's office. Mom agreed to listen to Joe, but I don't think she wants to go through with this. She told Donnie she's afraid Dad will be mad at her. Besides, she's not really convinced he's an alcoholic.

WE'RE GOING TO DO IT!

Joe convinced Mom that Dad was an alcoholic by reading her one of those ten-question tests. You know, Do You Drink in the Morning? Do You Drink Alone? Have You Ever Shot a Member of Your Family While Drinking? Those kind of questions. But Mom is still really afraid. If it doesn't work, she said, her life will be hell. Joe asked how her life was now, and she started to cry. So we're all aboard. We're all doing the intervention. Here's how it works. You surprise the alcoholic. He walks into a room filled with his friends and family and co-workers, whomever, and the counselor, in this case Joe. The counselor runs the intervention and tells the alcoholic why everyone is there and asks the alcoholic to sit and listen. Then each person tells the alcoholic how the alcoholic's drinking has impacted that person's life, and talks about two or three specific instances where the alcoholic made them feel bad or embarrassed or hurt or whatever. Joe says the important part is to talk about the feelings. Then someone tells the alcoholic that they want him to get treatment, and then everyone tells the alcoholic what will happen if he doesn't. You'll lose your job; or Dad, I won't talk to you anymore; or I'll ask for a divorce. But you have to really mean it. Everything has to be honest. Then the counselor asks the alcoholic to respond. And hopefully, he cries and says thank you and lets somebody drive him to the rehab where a bed has already been reserved. I'm scared.

BOTTOM THIS!

I'm in the basement. And feeling very codependent right now.
Mom, Donnie, and I have been walking around the house
kind of trying to avoid Dad, kind of watching him. Does he
suspect something? I'm walking on eggshells, feeling guilty,
then overwhelmed, then angry, then justified when Dad gets
tanked. I think shooting Donnie threw him for a loop. Maybe
this is Dad's bottom. Donnie went to an AA meeting today. He
said they were playing "Bottom This!," kind of a friendly com-
petition to see who had the worst bottom. Donnie's is pretty
good, but this guy named Roy took the prize. He said he was on
his porch last summer, drinking beer and eating potato chips. He
said that somehow one of his kids broke the porch light, knocking the broken bulb into his bowl of potato chips, and he was so
wasted he just ate the pieces of bulb, thinking they were chips.
Donnie said everyone in the meeting was roaring with laughter
as Roy described coughing up the blood and realizing that
maybe his life had become unmanageable. They say alcoholics
get help when they've hit bottom. So I think maybe we should
let Dad hit his own bottom. But then I realize that maybe my
mother sitting in a room with a counselor, telling Dad how his
drinking makes her feel, maybe for Dad that would be like eating a light bulb.

DAD'S RETIRED AND ALL HIS FRIENDS ARE DRUNKS!

Which Joe says makes things harder. Right now the only people in the room will be Joe and the immediate family. All we can really threaten is to break off our relationships with Dad. Although I know Mom isn't willing to do that. In fact, she couldn't think of any threat to make in the intervention. I think she's settled on one Joe suggested. If Dad refuses to stop drinking, she's going to spend less time taking care of him and more time pursuing her own interests. Not a lot of teeth in that threat, since Mom has no interests. Joe thinks the one who will have real impact on Dad is Donnie, since Donnie really is Dad's best friend and companion. As much as Donnie makes fun of Dad, he really, *really* loves him. And Dad knows it. So Joe seems to think that Donnie will be the key. Still, Joe asked us if there was anything else, any other leverage? Well, I said, Dad might be going to jail. Joe got all excited. We told him about the hearing and how Dad and Donnie face perjury charges. Joe said he'd talk to the judge. Maybe she'd throw out the charges if Dad agrees to get treatment. Joe said that of all the motivators to get someone to quit drinking and drugging, avoiding jail is usually the most dependable.

TODAY I CAN LET GO OF THE RESULT! II

The judge told Joe that she would being willing to drop the perjury charges against Donnie and Dad on two conditions. First, if they both agree to get treatment, which obviously is okay with Donnie. And secondly, if it's okay with the Egeberg estate. So later today I'm having coffee with Merle Egeberg. I feel this tremendous pressure to do this right, like Dad's life depends on how I do in this meeting. Talk about grandiosity! Well, I'm just going to do the best I can and let go of the result. But this time I mean it! Because sometimes when I promise myself to let go of the result, I don't, and I screw things up. And this time it's just too important!

TODAY I REMEMBER THAT THIS WORLD IS FULL OF GOOD PEOPLE!

Merle Egeberg is a wonderful person! We met at this coffee shop across the street from the Unitarian church where I attend my Al-Anon meetings. It turns out that Merle is very active in the church, and in fact, does a lot of organizing for food drives and helped set up a medical van that provides care for poor kids on the North Side. Merle was really curious about Al-Anon, and I talked and talked, as you can imagine, and went into the whole story about Aunt Paula, and well, just the whole saga. So, of course, it was okay with Merle that the judge drop the perjury charges. In fact, Merle offered to come to the intervention if it helped. I was so impressed with the kindness of this person! And the passion! Yes, passion! If you could have seen the conviction in those deep brown eyes as Merle talked about Hubert Humphrey! About how Hubert Humphrey said that a society should be judged by how well it takes care of youngest and its oldest and those who are handicapped or sick or disadvantaged. Those in the dawn of life, those in the dusk of life, and those in the shadows of life. And I told Merle how glad I was that we had coffee together and how I don't think I'd ever met a more passionate person. And Merle said, "Then you never met Hubert Humphrey." Oh, the intervention is tomorrow. Pearl Harbor Day! Tomorrow, the sneak attack on Dad.

You're Only As Sick As Your Secrets!

Last night I sat in the basement trying to think of what I'm going to talk about at the intervention. It's just four hours off, and I'm still not sure exactly what I'm going to say, but I think it'll be okay. Down in the basement I found some old pictures in a box, pictures that never found their way into a family album. An out-of-focus Donnie in a coonskin hat, Jodie on Dad's shoulders with her eyes shut, and I got kind of misty. Things weren't so bad. They did their best. Then I found a picture I thought Mom had thrown out. It was a picture of me, in Hollywood, getting hit by a car. I think it actually might be worth something. I mean, how many pictures exist of someone getting hit by a car at the exact moment of impact. It was our big trip to L.A. You know, Disneyland, the whole bit. I was about ten, and I think Aunt Paula helped pay for the trip. Anyway, on the last day, we were supposed to see Hollywood. Well, Dad got loaded the night before and by the time we got him up, we had about an hour to see Hollywood. So we drove down Hollywood Boulevard, and Dad would stop the car and we'd run out and look at the names on the sidewalk and jump back in. But Jodie kept saying she wanted a picture of her standing in front of the HOLLYWOOD sign, and Mom said we didn't have enough time and it was Dad's fault because he couldn't get up, which made Dad mad, so Dad promised Jodie he'd get a picture of her standing in front of the HOLLYWOOD sign. So Dad drove down Hollywood Boulevard till he could see the HOLLYWOOD sign, and we jumped out again, but the angle wasn't right for taking the picture. So we hopped back in and Dad started tearing around looking for a place to take the picture, and the next thing we were racing up the Hollywood Hills winding our way toward the sign. But whenever we jumped out, the angle wasn't right from the side of the road—there were always houses or trees blocking the sign—

and we'd jump back in. By now Mom and Dad were just screaming at each other, and all of us, including Jodie, said we should just forget the picture. But Dad said no, because he didn't want Mom saying that Jodie didn't get her picture in front of the HOLLYWOOD sign because he got up late. So we stopped again and we all piled out, and again the view of the sign was blocked from the side of the road. So Dad told us to get in the middle of the road. But there are cars, Dad! Just get out there! So we ran out, and Dad lined up the shot, and we'd hear a car coming around the curve and scurry back to side of the road, and Mom is screaming at Dad, and he's yelling at us to get back in the middle of the road, so we're running back and forth. And finally, Dad gets it all lined up. Quick! Get out here! And we run out, and Dad's looking through the camera, and Donnie hears the car and yells, but I guess I was so out of breath I just froze and Dad says, "Cheese!" and click, it's like the hardest thing in the world slams into me, and I'm flying through the air. The doctors in the emergency room said if I wasn't so fat I would really have gotten hurt. But the weird part is we've never talked about it since. In fact, in a way I think that's when the no-talk rule began in our household. From then on we didn't talk about anything bad. The good times were enshrined, like Mom's holiday meals, and the bad times forgotten. But at noon today when Donnie brings Dad to meet "his new lawyer," all that will end. Big time.

TODAY I WILL REMEMBER THAT ALCOHOLISM IS A CUNNING, BAFFLING, AND POWERFUL DISEASE! VII

Joe told us that interventions are staged early in the day, so chances are better that the alcoholic won't be drunk. Well, it worked. Dad wasn't drunk. In fact, once Dad walked in and figured out what was going on, he was more sober than I had seen him in years. Sober and *angry*. But controlled. It was as if his disease knew it was cornered, on trial for its life. And we were the hostile witnesses, and the only way to win its case was to destroy each of us. Jodie was first. I guess she opened herself up when she talked, or rather blubbered about how Dad got drunk at all her weddings. Dad, you might say, compared himself favorably to each of her husbands. "Dopey, Drunky, and Shithead," he called them, saying that at least he stayed with his ungrateful family and provided for us, and then he talked about Jodie and used the word "fat" a lot. Then it was my turn. I said there were a lot of instances in my childhood where Dad's drinking made me feel bad, but since this was now, I wanted to talk about now. I said, "Dad, I've changed a lot in the last few years, and it hurts me that you refuse to see it." And I started to cry, and Dad got all sarcastic, "I'm here for you, Stuart. C'mon, why don't you give your alcoholic Dad a big hug? Isn't that what you do in your twelve-step groups?" And then Dad said he was going to organize one of these for me because I was addicted, addicted to twelve-step programs. And I got so mad that I honestly didn't care whether this worked or not. Then Donnie. Donnie said, "Dad, I love you." Then he pulled up his shirt and showed Dad his bandages. He said, "Dad, we're both drunks. It's not your fault, and it's not mine. But you know what?" And I was still so mad I said, "Chicken butt." And everyone turned to me, and I apologized and Donnie went on. He told Dad he was dangerous, that the alcohol made him dangerous. To himself and to all of us. That he had scarred us all, not physical scars like the ones he'll have on his abdomen, but emotional scars. Then Donnie looked straight at Dad and said that he wasn't going to let Dad control our reality anymore. That stuff happened, and that we were always taught that we were crazy if we thought anything was wrong. And then he talked about another secret. When Donnie was a junior in high school, he was the starting pitcher for the baseball team. He could just throw that ball incredibly hard. He thought he had a good chance to be elected captain of the team. Well, Dad got really drunk at one of the games, and . . . oh God, he went down to the snack bar and he . . . Dad exposed himself. To one of the cheerleaders. A number of people saw it, and of course, it got around school, and . . . Well, in our house, anyway, it was never discussed. There was this awful silence, a silence that kind of summed up all the silences we had lived through all our lives. And then Dad just said it never happened. So we turned to Mom. C'mon, Mom. It happened, right? And we waited. And then Mom said, "Maybe if you just cut down a little. After the holidays." And Joe told Dad about the judge, and Dad said that the judge should go fuck herself, and then he walked out. So my feeling is that Dad is still probably going to object to my publishing this book.

TODAY I WILL LIVE MY LIFE!

Donnie and Jodie drove me to the airport. There was total silence until I finally blurted, "Well, that was a fun trip home!" We howled with laughter. And then in a way it was nice. For the moment, at least, the three of us basked in the warm glow of mutual failure. At least we had tried. We talked about how odd it's going to be not to have Christmas at Mom and Dad's. Donnie will be in rehab, his fifth. He says five's a charm. I invited Jodie and Kyle down to Chicago, but she says Kyle will be swimming, so she'll just make her own turkey. We laughed about Mom making the whole Christmas spread anyway. Hope Dad likes leftovers, if he's not already in jail. Me. I'll be getting on with my life. I called Mary, the Lifeline program director, when I got back in. She says my shows have been getting a good response. Julia's coming over tonight and we're going to talk about a series of shows around the subject, You're Only as Sick as Your Secrets. So, you see, everything's working out just great.

TODAY I WILL LIGHTEN UP!

Julia's background is even sicker than mine. As you might remember, the big secret in her childhood really was about who Julia is. Her father wasn't her biological father. Whenever Julia talks about it she gets kind of angry. And then bummed out. Which is good. At least she's feeling the feelings. So last night Julia told me a secret she'd never told anyone. Not in any meeting, not even to her sponsor. She told me that after getting into Al-Anon, she decided to get in contact with her real biological father. She wanted to find out who she really was. Her mom refused to tell her the man's name, but she did some investigative work and found out who he was and tracked him down. He lives in Joliet, about an hour from the city. Julia called him, and the man agreed to meet with her. So they had dinner in the city, and Julia said she could understand why her mom had been attracted to him. He was in his early fifties, handsome, and charming. He told her that he knew he had fathered this girl, but purposely stayed out of her life, but now that Julia had initiated contact, he'd like to see her more and develop a real relationship. Well, Julia saw him for dinner a couple of more times, and one night as they were leaving the restaurant her biological father put his arm around her and made a pass. Did I title this one "Today I Will Lighten Up!"? I'm sorry. I think I'm still reeling from what went on in Minnesota.

OKAY, *TODAY* I WILL LIGHTEN UP!

Julia and Carl and Steve and his wife came over last night, and we talked some more about secrets. Which on the face of it was dangerous considering Steve and Julia's history, but of course that's in the open because Steve's wife read his fourth step. So Carl asked Steve if he had any secrets remaining and Steve said, "Yes. It's a very dark secret. I've masturbated. Once. I mean tonight, since I got here." And we were all laughing. Then I told everyone about getting hit with the car in Hollywood, and they were howling. And you know what? It just felt good to laugh!

TODAY I AM A TOTALLY COMPETENT PERSON!

I feel strangely confident. Or strangely competent. Or just strange! Anyway, I'm taping today, and I feel good about it. But not cocky or grandiose. Steve calls it "delusions of adequacy." That's a joke. It's just that it feels like everything that's ever happened to me has brought me to this moment. And I guess that's something to remember. Which is that we can actually learn and benefit from all this bizarre stuff that happens to us. I am who I am, I don't want to trade places with anybody, and my experience has made me stronger. I am in recovery, hear me roar!

TODAY I WILL GO TO A MOVIE!

There's so much stuff I have to do. My laundry. Stop in while Walter edits my shows, which went great. I have to buy a book on being a best man. I have to make a list, then lose it! But you know what? I'm going to see a movie. And not one that will in any way broaden my horizons. I'm going to see a comedy. A comedy starring John Candy!

I'VE BEEN ASKED TO SPEAK AT THE
INTERNATIONAL SHAME CONFERENCE!!!!!!

Last night they aired the first of my "You're Only as Sick as Your Secrets" shows, entitled "Feeling Crazy and Being Crazy Are Two Different Things." Someone from the International Shame Conference saw it and called Mary, the program director at Lifeline, and asked if I would be interested in speaking on affirmations at the conference. *Would I be interested?!* Does Ted Kennedy have a drinking problem?! But, of course, I'm scared. The conference starts in four days! A speaker on deep breathing dropped out at the last minute, and they want me to replace her. Is this actually happening?! They're paying my plane to Los Angeles, hotel, and per diem for food, plus six hundred dollars. I must be dreaming! Of course, this could turn into a nightmare. Half the recovery community will be there. I'll feel like an imposter, like I have no right to be there and fall into a tremendous shame spiral. But then again, maybe not. I mean, this is a humongous opportunity. And life is about taking risks. I have to grab this opportunity and run with it. Oh, I forgot to tell you. John Bradshaw is the featured speaker at the conference! Somebody pinch me.

I AM WORTH PREPARING FOR!

Okay. I've been working straight through. Writing, viewing tapes. My own, and I borrowed Bradshaw's series on healing the inner child from Joanne. Oh, she and Bob broke up again. I've decided to pattern my presentation on Bradshaw's. Only more so. I mean, the man is a prophet! But I have to be careful to learn from him and be inspired by him, and not compare myself to him. So I've decided to go multimedia. Slides, overhead projector, audiotapes, music, videotape, light cues. I want this to be really dramatic! Walter, who is a genius, is doing all the tech. Steve has volunteered his advertising agency to help with graphics, video editing, etc. My juices are flowing! Now, one of the most moving sequences in Bradshaw's lecture is this videotape he shows of anger work at his family therapy institute. In the tape the person holds a red padded bat called the battaca bat, and as a counselor guides this person through their anger, usually at a parent, the person really feels his or her anger and pounds away at the pillow, screaming in rage. It's a great release, a healthy way to get at and express the anger you may not have realized was really there. I wish I had one of those bats in Minnesota! Anyway, I have this theory, which is that if you combined this exercise with a daily affirmation, screaming *"I am good enough! I am smart enough!"* while pounding the pillow, it might use the energy or e-motion, as Bradshaw calls it, of the anger exercise to reinforce the affirmation. Really drive that affirmation home! So today we're doing a little videotaping. Now, I am not a licensed therapist, so I'm doing this with friends. Carl, Julia, Steve, Joanne, and some of Joanne's friends. This is powerful stuff, and I don't want to ruin anyone's life.

I AM NOT A LICENSED THERAPIST.

The battaca-bat affirmation experiment was a success. Well, actually there were mixed results. First of all, the women seemed much more able than the men to get at their anger. Julia was scary. I just kept telling her the pillow was her father. But by far the most savage rage came out of Joanne. But she had a hard time doing the affirmation along with it. Mainly she kept screaming, "Bob, you fucking son of a bitch!" The men had more difficulty. Steve just couldn't hit the pillow no matter how hard I tried to get him angry. I role-played his mother, "You're a genius, Steve! I expect you to be the smartest person wherever you are, and if you're not, you're no good!" But Steve just couldn't do it, and he apologized and gave me the bat back. By far, the worst failure was Russ, Joanne's new boyfriend, who I don't think wanted to be there. Joanne told me Russ's father always wanted him to be a football player, but Russ hated football. So as Russ knelt in front of his pillow, bat in hand, I kept saying, "This is your father, Russ! C'mon, get a touchdown! What's wrong with you!? Tackle that guy!" and Russ just sat there and said he wasn't getting in touch with his anger, but it seemed to me he was. He was getting angrier and angrier. So I kept going, "What's wrong with you? Get out there and hit, son!" And Russ told me to stop. But I thought he was just about to explode. So I kept egging him on. "What are you? A sissy?! Kill those guys! Kick their ass!" And Russ did explode. On me! He kept hitting me with the bat, screaming, "You're not a licensed therapist! You're not a licensed therapist!"

I HAVE PUT COMPETENT PEOPLE IN MY LIFE!

I leave for Los Angeles this afternoon. Everything's been so rushed I haven't had time to worry. Which is maybe good. Steve thinks I might have overcomplicated my show. That maybe I'm overcompensating for the fact that I don't believe I that I really have enough to say. That I feel like a fraud in the midst of all these recovery professionals and that I feel I need all this glitz to impress them. He thinks maybe I should maybe just get up there and talk, and I told him it's too late now. My whole lecture is built around these slides and audiotapes and the videotape of Julia hitting the pillow with the bat. Steve said he's just worried that if something goes wrong technically, I'll be thrown. And I told him I'd worry about that too. If it wasn't for Walter. The man is a whiz. We've been rehearsing with all the different cues, and he's been right on the money. There's still a lot of fine-tuning to do, but Walter called ahead to the conference and we can rehear— Ooops, the phone! . . . Hello? . . . Oh, hi, Walter, I was just . . . Oh, God, that's terrible. . . . No, no, you should definitely stay. . . . I hope she makes it. . . . No, it's okay. This is my fault; I did this to myself. . . . A substitute? . . . Glenn? Is he good? . . . Gee, there's so much to learn. . . . So you recommend h— Well, what can I say? I'm desperate!

I Am a Fool! IV or V

Okay. This is the low point. I've brought an active alcoholic to the International Shame Conference! Oh, Glenn seems technically competent. In fact, when I met him at O'Hare he seemed great. I brought all my tapes and slides and stuff and Glenn stopped me from putting the videotapes through the X-ray machine. Which would have been a disaster, after all that work. What am I talking about? This is a disaster! Glenn got drunk on the plane. In fact, I think I figured out why he agreed to do this. He thought this was a convention. You know, booze and broads. I mean, last night, we get into the hotel, he heads right to the bar, which was empty, and starts yelling "Where is everybody?!" and downs four or five tequilas, and then get this! He staggers out through the lobby into a conference room and hits on the leader of the incest survivor group! So he was too drunk to rehearse. And my entire presentation is in this guy's hands. But that's okay. Because I deserve this. Okay? I deserve this! Why did I believe for one minute that I had anything to tell these people? They're recovery professionals! John Bradshaw is here! I saw him last night, walking through the lobby. I almost went up to talk to him, but, well, I was too embarrassed. I think everyone knows I'm the guy who brought the drunk. I called Carl to make an amends for being here instead of working on his bachelor party, and he told me I was in a shame spiral and that I should take this a day at a time and work on a presentation without all the technical stuff, and that who knows, maybe Glenn will sleep it off and be of some use. Right!

IT'S OKAY TO WANT WHAT YOU WANT!

Okay. Glenn slept late yesterday, but when he finally woke up, he was very apologetic. In fact, he was embarrassed, and I felt a little bad for him. So I told him that he shouldn't feel bad and that, in fact, this is the International Shame Conference, so this is the last place he needs to feel ashamed. If only I believed that myself! Anyway, Glenn and I did rehearse today, and he did pretty well considering he had a bad hangover. Then we viewed my battaca-bat sessions, and I picked the take I want to go with. It's Julia yelling, "I deserve to be treated with respect!" at her father, and it's actually a very cathartic moment. So Glenn cued it to that point, and that's what we're going to play. And then I went to John Bradshaw's lecture at the convention center across the street, because about six thousand people came, and he was amazing. He made me laugh; he made me cry. And at one point he said something that made me feel better about being here. He said, "It's okay to want what you want. There's nothing you should or should not want. If you're in touch with your life energy, you will want to expand and grow. It's okay and necessary to get your needs met." And I realized . . . I want to do this! This! I want to help people get rid of their Critical Inner Voice, or at least answer it with something positive! Then like an idiot I started to compare my presentation with Bradshaw's and I started to spiral again. But that's okay! Progress, not perfection. Anyway, my presentation is this evening. It's in a small ballroom and I doubt anyone will come. But that's okay! In fact, I prefer it. Because it's probably not going to be very good. Okay. I think I'll go to Glenn's room and try to wake him up for rehearsal.

I AM A HUMAN BEING!

Glenn was fine in run-through. In fact, all the cues were so perfect, it made me nervous. Evidently, it made him nervous too. Because he started to drink and didn't stop until he was shit-faced. When he came back from the bar, I just looked at him and thought, "That's my Dad! My Dad is in control of my life!" and I went into this spin unlike any spin, because . . . I had done it again. I had put myself in the hands of an active alcoholic! So, as the chairman of the National Shame Conference was introducing me to about five hundred people, five hundred recovery professionals, all of whom know more about this stuff than I ever will, I looked out at the control board and saw my Dad controlling my destiny. "Our next speaker has his own television show"—Great, I thought, I'm the twelve-step Jimmy Swaggert—"and is currently writing a book on daily affirmations, entitled *I'm Good Enough, I'm Smart Enough, and Doggone it, People Like Me!*" (Hubris! Hubris! I'm thinking, hubris and giant gobs of irony!) "And he's here to talk on the subject, 'Daily Affirmations: Shame's Worst Nightmare.' Please welcome Stuart Smalley." Walking out there was like facing the jury on a murder rap. And you knew you were guilty. But the first cue came up! My music! On cue! "I'm going to do a great lecture today"—the words were actually coming out of my mouth—"because I'm good enough, I'm smart enough, and gosh darn it, people like me!" And then I talked about how my Critical Inner Voice is always there, sitting inside my brain, and the slide came up, right on cue, depicting the little Critical Inner Voice inside my skull. My God! This is working! And it was. They liked me. They really did. But then things started going South. Fast. Glenn played the wrong music, then pressed reverse on the slide tray, and I fell apart. My mind floated up to the ceiling and watched my body panic. I forgot where I was, I repeated myself.

I could feel them staring at me. And then the big moment. My battaca/affirmation breakthrough. I recited my theory, how the energy of the battaca exercise could reinforce the affirmation and vice versa, and turned everyone's attention to the huge video screen. It was Russ. Joanne's new boyfriend. "C'mon, stop it," he was saying. And I yelled back, "What are you? A sissy?! Kill those guys! Kick their ass!" Glenn had forgotten to recue the tape. I just froze. And watched, along with the five hundred recovery professionals, as Russ pounded the shit out of me, screaming, "You're not a licensed therapist! You're not a licensed therapist!" I ran from the room, into the hallway, bent over, hyperventilating. The low point of my life! And then I heard the voice. "It's okay, Stuart. It's okay." I looked up, and there he was. John Bradshaw. John Bradshaw had witnessed this, this ultimate humiliation. But he was saying it was okay. "Hey, let's not forget why we're here. All of us, everyone of us at this conference, knows what you're feeling, because all of us have been there ourselves." "But you don't understand, Mr. Bradshaw, you're my hero!" "Stuart, by making me more than human, you're making yourself less than human. And Stuart, you're a human being. And you are good enough, you are smart enough, and doggone it, people like you." And, of course, I realized he was right. And as I looked into his eyes, I felt the acceptance, the unconditional acceptance that I knew was awaiting me in that room. So we marched back, me and John, and I finished my presentation, and I don't know what I said, but when I finished I received a standing ovation!

IT'S OKAY TO BASK!

used to believe that if you accomplished something, really achieved something significant, it was time to worry about the next thing. In other words, better not celebrate. Because if you do, everything's going to fall apart. Well, today I am basking in the afterglow of what I now refer to as The Triumph in L.A.! Get this. I even used my frequent flyer miles to upgrade myself to first class! It was my way of saying "Congratulations, Stuart, job well done!" Also, I didn't have to sit next to Glenn.

JODIE'S IN REHAB!

Sometimes codependents have trouble making decisions. Especially when they're also addicted to pain pills and Valium. So I guess when Jodie was on the train tracks and saw the train coming, she couldn't decide whether to back up or go forward. Of course, either decision would have been a good one. Luckily, Kyle made it for her, jumping over to put the car into reverse, just in time. The train clipped the front bumper, and Kyle dislocated his shoulder, but Jodie came out okay. Except that she called Joe, who got her a bed at Hazelden. So I'm back in Minneapolis. I guess you could say the intervention worked after all.

TODAY IT'S OKAY TO BE QUIET.

Jodie was lucky to get a bed right away. Although according to Joe, late December is a little slow for rehabs. Most alcoholics and addicts like to have their big holiday binge before checking themselves in after the first of the year. Jodie has five days of detox, then about a week in rehab before we're allowed to see her. So that's next year. In the meantime, I can't really get Kyle to talk about anything. How he feels about his mom being away. How he feels about his shoulder and not swimming for a while. How he feels about having Christmas with me in Chicago. But for now, that's okay!

I Can Set Priorities!

When Kyle got to my apartment, he just looked around and said, "So this is where I'm going to live from now on." And I realized that for a boy who's seen two fathers leave him, this has got to be kind of scary. So I said, "No, Mom's just a little sick, and she's gone to the hospital to get better. And when she gets back, she'll be back forever. And also she'll be a lot less nervous. Does that sound good?" And Kyle nodded, I think especially at the lot-less-nervous part. And then we settled in. We flipped for the bed and Kyle won, so it's the couch for me. Today I was going to start making the arrangements for Carl's bachelor party. I feel so guilty that I haven't done anything. But you know what? I called Carl and told him what's going on, and he agreed with me. In fact, I think this is the first time he ever gave me direct advice. He said forget the bachelor party and buy a Christmas tree. So that's my priority for today. Kyle and I are going to buy the biggest tree we can find, and we're going to trim it, and at some point I'm going to call Julia and ask her to go out and buy Kyle an Intendo or Nintendo or whatever those things are!

ALCOHOLISM IS A THREEFOLD DISEASE: THANKSGIVING, CHRISTMAS, AND NEW YEAR'S!

It's about five in the morning and Kyle's still asleep. And I'm thinking what a lousy Christmas for an eight-year-old kid. But then again, Christmas has always been lousy. The whole holiday season. You know, I've always thought this Norman Rockwell image of the holidays created a lot of unrealistic expectations. In fact, sometimes around this time of year, I get this fantasy of seeing Norman Rockwell in one of the meeting rooms, standing up and saying, "My name is Norman, and I paint lies!" And living up to these expectations, or trying to appear to live up to them, was always a lot of work. One of the great Christmas traditions in the Smalley household was the Christmas Eve shouting match about who wasn't helping out enough. Well, Kyle should be up soon. And Julia did buy him a whole lot of presents. And if he's like most eight-year-old kids I know, that should help!

MY FRIENDS ENRICH MY LIFE!

This turned out to be a very nice Christmas. And all because I have made some great friends this year. Julia was a hero! The toys were a smash, and she even bought loads of batteries. In the morning Kyle and I played Nintendo, and I discovered that this kid does not like to lose, which is very COA. Whenever his Mario guy would get killed or whatever, Kyle would scream, "That's not fair!" But I think I made him feel a little better, because I was so hopelessly bad. Then we went over to Steve's house, where they celebrate both Hanukkah and Christmas. In fact, I asked his little five-year-old, Jenny, what the advantage of being half Jewish and half Christian was, thinking she'd say she gets to celebrate both holidays, but she said, "If someone asks you if you're Jewish, you can say 'no.'" Steve just rolled his eyes and said, "That's my mother-in-law talking." And then he told Jenny to be proud of who she is, and that she shouldn't hesitate to tell anyone she's Jewish, unless they're on a plane overseas and get hijacked. Anyway, Steve and his kids and me and Kyle went down to a soup kitchen, which was Steve's idea, because he wanted to show his kids the real meaning of Christmas, and I guess a lot of other people had the same idea, because there were about forty of us serving about twenty homeless people. And it reminded me of something that Merle Egeberg told me, which is that most of us think about and give to the needy during the holiday season, but that these people need to eat every day of the year. And then we went back to Steve's and stuffed ourselves! Caroline made a beautiful turkey, and everything was delicious! But Kyle was still kind of quiet. Which is understandable. Steve and Caroline are strangers to Kyle, and their kids are younger. Which brings me to the best part. We got home, and there was a message on the machine. "Hey, Stuart. You know what? Chicken butt!" It was Brent. He and his parents are staying at his uncle's in Elgin. I can't wait to get these kids together!

EVERY DAY BRINGS A CHANCE FOR RENEWAL!

Julia came over yesterday morning to drive me and Kyle out to Elgin. Just as we were about to leave, Kyle's father called, which I thought was kind of odd, considering Jodie told me he hadn't talked to Kyle in about three years. So I assumed he was going to offer to take Kyle while Jodie was in rehab, which I thought would be a bad idea. But I put Kyle on the phone anyway, and then I heard Kyle say, "No. My birthday's June 26. . . . Yeah, I'm eight. . . . Bye." Kyle looked pretty glum, so I asked him what that was about, and he said his dad had found an old cash card and he had used Kyle's birthday as his code word, and he wanted to see if there was any money left in the account. So I asked Kyle how he felt about that, and he shrugged and he said he didn't know, but he started to cry, and then he reached out and hugged me. When he let go, I said, "Kyle, do you still want to go meet Brent?" And he nodded yeah, so we drove out, and when we got to Elgin, Brent was in the living room with his mom, who was just wrapping up his stretching exercises. And Brent asked Kyle if he wanted to know what the stretching exercises were for and Kyle said yeah, and then Brent explained how he has dead muscle tissue and this was to keep it from tightening up. And when he was finished, he showed Kyle his new Nintendo, which was the same one Kyle got, so they started playing, only this time when his Mario got killed, Kyle didn't yell "That's not fair!" So anyway, the adults went into the kitchen. And as we were having coffee, we started hearing these giggles and screams from the living room. So we went in there and asked what they were up to, and Kyle said they were just goofing off. So we went back to our coffee, and about twenty minutes later, a remote control car came skidding into the kitchen with a note attached. The note said, "Is it okay if Kyle stays overnight?" Well, of course it was okay. And when we went out in the living room to say so, Kyle grinned at me and said, "You know what?!" And I said, "What?" And they both screamed "Chicken butt!" and fell down laughing. Well, Brent was already down.

I AM A GOOD INFLUENCE!

The bachelor party is tonight. After the rehearsal dinner. Carl's friend Ernie has been covering for me. He reserved a room in this health food restaurant, and invited all of Carl's male friends. And I can't believe it. We're actually going to have a woman jump out of the cake! Which is not like Carl or any of his friends, all of whom would consider it sexist and exploitative and dehumanizing. But Eileen from our Tuesday OA meeting *wants* to do it. She's down about eighty pounds from a good two-twenty and she's very proud of her body right now. So I guess we're going to go wild. Meanwhile, Andrea's family has come to town, and Carl can't believe it. Her father drove in from Detroit with a date, a woman at least forty years his junior. Which is driving Andrea's mother crazy, which, of course, it was designed to do. Although I'm sure she was already crazy. The woman weighs at least three hundred pounds, and already half of the wedding party has tried to twelve-step her. And Andrea! Oh, Andrea looks so beautiful! She's lost one hundred and sixty-seven pounds! Carl and Andrea are flying to Hawaii after the wedding. And get this. On New Year's Day Andrea is going to start the new year by running, swimming, and biking in the Hawaiian Tropic Triathlon! My editor. And she says she owes it all to me!

I'M ALMOST DONE WITH THE BOOK!

I've been so busy lately, I really totally forgot that I'm almost done doing this. And I have lots of feelings about it. First of all, I feel like I'm forgetting to tell you about the bachelor party, which was a lot of fun. And Eileen looked great! I mean, she did a really hot dance! I mean, we were surprised! I mean, I was really surprised, because I brought Kyle and Brent and, well, I don't think it hurt them any. In fact, they've been giggling about it all day. Brent's folks let me use their van. It's got a hydraulic lift for Brent. Anyway, I've been running around town getting stuff ready for the wedding. One of my jobs, of course, is decorating the getaway car. How's this? Instead of "Just Married," I was thinking of "Just Happy" or "Just Grateful." But I don't know. Brent thought of "Just Kidding." Well, I still have a few hours to think of a good one. Oh, my feelings about the book. First of all, I'm a little scared. I haven't reread it yet, and I'm sure it's horrible. Then I'm also a little sad, because I think this has been a good process for me, and I'm going to miss it. But then again, I could keep doing it, but it wouldn't have the same urgency, which shouldn't make any difference . . . but anyway. Oh, also I worry about not having a good ending. Because I feel like the book should end in some great way. But, you know, tomorrow I'll talk about the wedding, which is climactic, I know. But then it'll be December 31st and I'll write something about . . . something. Anyway, it's all okay. And today's the wedding! Oh, my God, I have to think of a toast!

I AM READY!

I liked Steve's toast better than mine. His was "May Carl's loins shoot fire, and Andrea's womb bear fruit!" Which everyone thought was funny! For my toast I was going to recite the Kahlil Gibran poem about two trees growing together, but far enough apart not to be in each other's shadow, but the maid of honor beat me to it. So I just spoke from my heart, which is always the best thing to do anyway, and well . . . the whole thing was so overwhelming. I mean, the love in that chapel during that ceremony! Everyone was crying. I even saw Andrea's mom smile at Andrea's dad as he led her down the aisle. And the music! Andrea's sister, who happens to be a big opera singer, sang this Beatles song, "In My Life," and, God, everyone was just bawling. Even the president of Dell, who is a wonderful man! Although I don't think he is that familiar with my book. Anyway, as Andrea walked down that aisle, all eyes were on her (and she was luminous), but not mine. I was looking at Carl, grinning from ear to ear. And she was looking at him, too; obviously, she couldn't be looking at herself. So I watched them looking at each other, as if sharing this happy secret. A secret called true intimacy. And it was at that moment that I decided how to end this book. Because it is time for me now. I am ready to let myself take the risk. I am strong enough now to be available for intimacy, to grow close to someone special without losing myself. I am ready to date!

I WILL CHOOSE HEALTHY, KIND, AND EMOTIONALLY AVAILABLE PEOPLE!

I called Merle last night, and we talked and talked. Somehow it seems as if we've known each other forever. Anyway, Kyle and I are flying into Minneapolis today. It should be a great New Year's Eve! Oh. Kyle told me last night that when he grows up he wants to be a doctor.

TODAY I WILL NOT JUMP AHEAD AND READ THE LAST PAGE OF A BOOK!

I'm only cheating myself when I do that!

I owe a tremendous debt of gratitude to so many people who helped me find the Stuart inside myself. First to all my colleagues at Saturday Night Live, especially Lorne Michaels and Jim Downey, who put Stuart on the air; Bonnie Turner who told me that Stuart was not a licensed therapist; Melina Root who found Stuart's sweater; and Gloria Rivera who found his hair. My book agent Jonathon Lazear, who sold the thing really quickly to Dell and got me a good deal. Oh, Jonathon also read the book as I went along and was tremendously encouraging. To Bonnie Dickel who suggested I call Jonathon in the first place. To Leslie Schnur, my editor, who is not Andrea, the character in the book, except that she is in a way, because she's smart and energetic and has been of tremendous help. Also she laughs a lot which is of monumental importance to me. To Melody Beattie, who moves me with her courage and generosity of spirit, and who also laughs a lot. To Elaine and Brian Fuller who gave me inspiration even when I didn't need it. To Bob Danielsen, my pal and my authority on Minnesota Probate Law. To George Vroom, Bob Gunn, and Ann Smith, all licensed therapists, who helped in very different ways, but I lumped them together because they're professionals. To all the friends of Lois W., most of whom I like, and all of whom I love in a special way. To the Bryson family, Fran, Cathy, Carla, Neal, and Phyllis, also known as my in-laws, all of whom I like and love, and who gave me some great stories. To my parents, Joe and Phoebe, who are nothing like Stuart's parents, honest. No son has had parents root for him harder. To my brother Owen, who really had nothing to do with this book, but he'd kill me if I left him out. To my kids, Thomasin and Joe, who don't let me kiss them as much as I would like, and who stayed up past midnight to watch me type the final affirmation so we could celebrate. And most of all to Franni, my wife.